Houghton
Mifflin
Harcourt

PERFORMANCE ASSESSMENT

3

Printed in the U.S.A.

ISBN 978-0-544-46520-6

15 0928 20 19 18

4500706873   A B C D E F G

Welcome Students,

The more you practice something, the better you get at it. With *Performance Assessment*, you will have the chance to practice reading and writing

- ▶ **opinion essays**
- ▶ **informative essays**
- ▶ **literary analysis**
- ▶ **narratives**

In each unit, you will master one of these types of writing by following three simple steps.

- ▶ **Analyze the Model**
- ▶ **Practice the Task**
- ▶ **Perform the Task**

As you follow these steps, you'll find yourself building the confidence you need to succeed at performance assessments. Let's get started!

Unit 1 Opinion Essay
All About Pets

Step 1 • Analyze the Model

Should people keep birds as pets?

Step 2 • Practice the Task

Should pets be allowed in school?

Step 3 • Perform the Task

Which are better: cats or dogs?

Read Source Materials

Unit 2 Informative Essay
250 Years Ago

Step 1 • Analyze the Model

How did American Indians' surroundings affect the way they lived?

Read Source Materials

Step 2 • Practice the Task

How did colonists travel in America?

Read Source Materials

Step 3 • Perform the Task

What was everyday life like for children in colonial America?

Read Source Materials

Unit 3 Response To Literature
Animal Tricksters

Step 1 • Analyze the Model

How do a character's actions drive the events of a story?

Read Source Materials

Step 2 • Practice the Task

How does a trickster get what he wants?

Read Source Materials

Step 3 Perform the Task

What are the character traits of a trickster?

Read Source Materials

Unit 4 Narrative
Strange Situations

Step 1 • Analyze the Model

What happens when cell phones don't work?

Read Source Materials

Step 2 • Practice the Task

What happens when an ostrich visits your house?

Read Source Materials

Step 3 Perform the Task

What happens when you develop an animal's abilities?

Read Source Materials

© Houghton Mifflin Harcourt Publishing Company • Image Credits: © Maria Gritsai/ Alamy

Unit 5 Mixed Practice
On Your Own

Task 1 • Opinion Essay
Research Simulation

Read Source Materials

Write an Opinion Essay

Task 2 • Informative Essay
Research Simulation

Read Source Materials

Write an Informative Essay

Task 3 • Response to Literature

Read Source Materials

Excerpt From a Novel

Write a Response to Literature

Task 4 • Narrative
Research Simulation

Read Source Materials

Informational Article

Informational Article

Write a Narrative

All About Pets

Unit 1

Opinion Essay

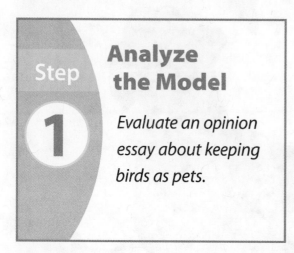

Step 1 — Analyze the Model

Evaluate an opinion essay about keeping birds as pets.

Step 2 — Practice the Task

Write an opinion essay about whether pets should be allowed in school.

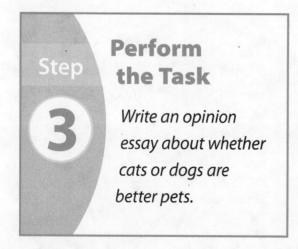

Step 3 — Perform the Task

Write an opinion essay about whether cats or dogs are better pets.

Everyone has opinions. What's an opinion? An opinion is a judgment you make about something. You may think that you should be able to stay up later. That is your opinion. Your parents may not share the same opinion.

IN THIS UNIT, you will learn how to write an opinion essay. Your essay will be based on your close reading and examination of sources. You will learn how to state an opinion and how to organize your essay in a clear way that makes sense to the reader.

Should people keep birds as pets?

You will read:

- **A School Magazine Article**
  Free Flying

- **An Advertisement**
  Feathered Friends Pet Shop

- **A Letter**
  from Allie

You will analyze:

- **A Student Model**
  Caged Birds Can't Fly

Unit 1: Opinion Essay

Source 1: School Magazine Article

This school magazine article was used by Mr. Lubov's student, Eddie Bao, as one of the sources for his essay, "Caged Birds Can't Fly." As you read, make notes in the side columns. Underline information that you find useful.

Notes

The Lincoln School Sixth Grade Monthly

Free Flying

By Estela Carranza

Birds are beautiful animals. You can see some kinds of birds flying high in the sky. Birds can make their nests in trees, in the ground, and even on the sides of cliffs! When a bird is caged, it doesn't have a nest to share with other birds. It cannot fly. Imagine being a bird and being unable to spread your wings. It is a sad thing to think about.

Most birds are social animals, so a bird in a cage can be lonely without other birds around. Some birds live to be 15 to 70 years old. That's a long time to be in a cage, especially if their owners don't have time to care for them.

1. Analyze   2. Practice   3. Perform

Pet birds need a lot of attention. In a cage, they can get bored because there isn't a lot to do. Birds will show that they are unhappy. Sometimes they will pull out their feathers. Some birds will walk quickly back and forth in their cages.

People can teach pet birds tricks. For example, some birds learn to repeat things that people say. This may be fun to show your friends, but is it fair? Do birds really want to learn human words?

Birds don't need to be in cages for you to enjoy them. Maybe you will see a bird if you look out your window. You can see pictures of birds on the Internet or in books. You can learn about different kinds of birds on TV and see them in their natural environment. Let the birds fly free!

© Houghton Mifflin Harcourt Publishing Company • Image Credits: © fotoVoyager/iStockPhoto.com

Discuss and Decide

Why can birds get bored in cages?

Source 2: Advertisement

Eddie used this advertisement as a second source for his essay. Continue to make notes in the side columns as you read. Underline information that you find helpful.

Notes

Feathered Friends Pet Shop

Birds make great pets! They are colorful, funny, and smart. You can train them to talk and do tricks!

We care for our birds and raise them here. Come in and see how happy and tame they are!

We sell:	We have:
• Finches	• Cages
• Parakeets	• Food
• Lovebirds	• Toys

Come in on the weekend for vet care and grooming—just for birds!

1. Analyze   2. Practice   3. Perform

OPEN 7 DAYS, 9:30 A.M. to 9 P.M.

1111 Warbler Drive,
at the corner of Beak Street

905-555-7387

www.featheredfriendspetshop.com

Serving the
bird community
since 1991

Close Read

According to the advertisement, why do birds make great pets?

Source 3: Letter

Eddie used this letter as a third source for his essay.
Continue to make notes in the side columns as you read.
Underline information that you find helpful.

Notes

Dear Suzie,

My parents got me a parakeet for my birthday! Parakeets are also called budgies. How great is that! He is very smart. He only knows a few words now, but I will teach him more.

Here he is!

1. Analyze   2. Practice   3. Perform

We put him in a *big cage* so he has room to move around. He won't hit the bars with his wings. We make sure to take him out of the cage when I get home from school. Boy, does he make a mess when he is outside the cage!

He is my responsibility, and I know I can take good care of him. I hope you can meet him soon!

Your friend,

Allie

Discuss and Decide

You have read three sources about keeping birds as pets. Without reading any further, discuss the question: Should people keep birds as pets?

Notes

Analyze a Student Model

Read Eddie's opinion essay closely. The red side notes are the comments that his teacher, Mr. Lubov, wrote.

Eddie Bao

March 22

Caged Birds Can't Fly

Clearly stated opinion, good work!

Birds are not meant to live in cages. Even if you take good care of a bird, being in a cage is bad for a bird's health.

Most birds want to fly, and a bird in a cage can't fly. We don't keep cats and dogs in cages. Yes, birds can be messy when they're out of their cages. But we can let them fly around inside! They need space to fly.

This would be a good place to use connecting words like "as a result" and "for instance."

Birds in cages are lonely as they cannot play or talk to other birds. They show that they are unhappy in cages. They pull out their feathers. They get bored in cages. There is nothing for them to do.

Birds can be a big responsibility because they can live a long time. Up to 70 years is a long time to take care of a pet! People need to think about how long they want to have a pet. Being responsible means thinking about how long you can care for a pet before you get one. You want to have responsibility to give care because that will help your pet.

Can you make this sentence clearer?

People can teach their birds to do tricks. Watching them makes people happy. These are good things about owning birds. But that does not mean we should make them pets.

This concluding section could be stronger.

Discuss and Decide

Does Eddie convince you that birds shouldn't be kept as pets? If so, cite evidence from his essay that makes you think so. If he doesn't convince you, why not?

Be Clear!

When you write, always check your work. Did you write what you meant to say? In his essay, Eddie could have stated some of his ideas more clearly.

Here is a confusing sentence from Eddie's essay:

> You want to have responsibility to give care because that will help your pet.

How could Eddie make his ideas clearer? He could state them in a more simple way. Here's an example:

> You need to be responsible for your pet and give it the care it needs.

Essay Tips

Remember These Tips When Writing!

- Read a sentence out loud if you are not sure it sounds right. Would your teacher write it the same way?

- Have a friend look at what you wrote. Does your friend understand what you mean?

Look back through Eddie's essay. Find one sentence that you could improve and underline it. Then rewrite the sentence so that it is more clear. Exchange your work with a partner. Ask your partner if what you wrote is easier to understand than what Eddie wrote.

_____

_____

Should pets be allowed in school?

You will read:

- **A Parent Letter**
  from Levi Hoffman, D.V.M.

- **A Student Letter**
  from Abigail

- **A Pet Policy**
  Pets in School: Our Classroom Rules

- **An Infographic**
  Handle with Care

You will write:

- **An Opinion Essay**
  Should pets be allowed in school?

Source 1: Parent Letter

AS YOU READ Analyze the letter. Note information that helps you decide where you stand on the issue: Should pets be allowed in school?

West Seattle
Veterinary Services
676 East McGraw St. #3H
West Seattle, WA 98116

Frederick McKenna, Principal
Seattle Elementary
800 Anderson Avenue
Seattle, WA 98111

Dear Principal McKenna,

My son David showed me the school's new policy for pets on school grounds. I am disappointed in your decision to keep pets out of school. I am a veterinarian, and I believe that animals have quite a lot to teach us human beings. There are many reasons to allow animals in school. Here are some of them.

1. Analyze   **2. Practice**   3. Perform

Animals teach us science and math. When I was in school, we raised baby chicks from eggs to learn about a chicken's life cycle. We counted how much food our pet rabbit ate, and we recorded his sleeping habits. Without pets, this type of up-close learning is not possible.

Animals build character. By taking care of animals, children learn responsibility. When they understand that pets depend on them to survive, they learn how to be gentle and kind.

Animals make kids feel better. Animals know what we need and give us a lot of love. They always seem to connect with us.

I hope that you will reconsider your school's pet policy.

Sincerely,

Levi Hoffman, D.V.M.

Discuss and Decide

What are two things Dr. Hoffman learned from animals?

Source 2: Student Letter

AS YOU READ Analyze the student letter. Note information that helps you decide where you stand on the issue: Should pets be allowed in school?

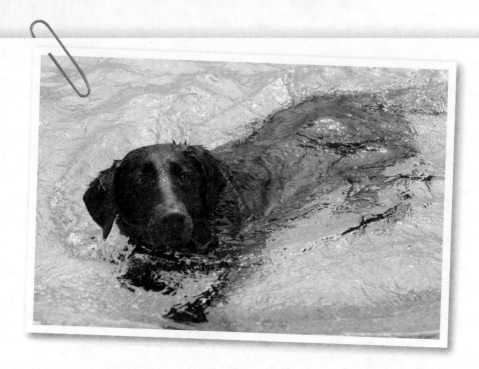

Dear Mrs. Zavikowski,

I know our school has rules, but I am writing to ask if I could bring my dog Cocoa in for show and tell. Cocoa is a chocolate Labrador, and she's my best friend!

I have looked online and I have learned that pets can be very good for our health. Pet owners have less stress and are more likely to talk to other people and be social. People with pets tend to be more active, too. This is information I want to share with the class.

1. Analyze   2. Practice   3. Perform

Cocoa is three years old. She is a good dog. I have taught her to sit, stay, and come. I know some people worry that dogs are not clean. But Cocoa is not very messy. I promise to keep her on a leash and away from the sandbox!

Thank you, Mrs. Zavikowski.

Sincerely,

Abigail

Close Read

What opposing opinion does Abigail address in her letter?

_____

_____

_____

_____

Source 3: Pet Policy

AS YOU READ Analyze the pet policy. Note information that helps you decide where you stand on the issue: Should pets be allowed in school?

Pets in School
Our Classroom Rules

We DO NOT allow:

- Wild animals, such as foxes or raccoons
- Poisonous animals, such as snakes or spiders
- Stray animals
- Baby chicks and ducklings
- Any animal that acts in a threatening way

We DO allow:

- Small pet rodents, such as mice or gerbils
- Pet rabbits
- Fish in an aquarium
- Birds like canaries, finches, or doves

If we take our animal out of a cage:

- We clean up after it.
- We do not play rough or tease.
- We do not feed it from our hands.
- We do not hold it close to our faces.
- We do not put our fingers close to its mouth.
- We are always gentle!

1. Analyze **2. Practice** 3. Perform

We allow these animals to visit:

- Healthy dogs, cats, and ferrets (always on a leash!)
- Guide dogs and service animals

Special Rules:

- If an animal seems scared or upset, we leave it alone.
- We always wash our hands after handling an animal.
- We always call the teacher (right away!) if a student or animal gets hurt.
- Our animal must live in its own home.
- We never touch animals until we're told it's okay.
- We never let our animal near an area where we wash or eat.
- We do not allow cats or dogs in the sandbox.

Discuss and Decide

Why is it important for students to wash their hands after handling an animal?

Source 4: Infographic

AS YOU READ Analyze the infographic. Note information that helps you decide where you stand on the issue: Should pets be allowed in school?

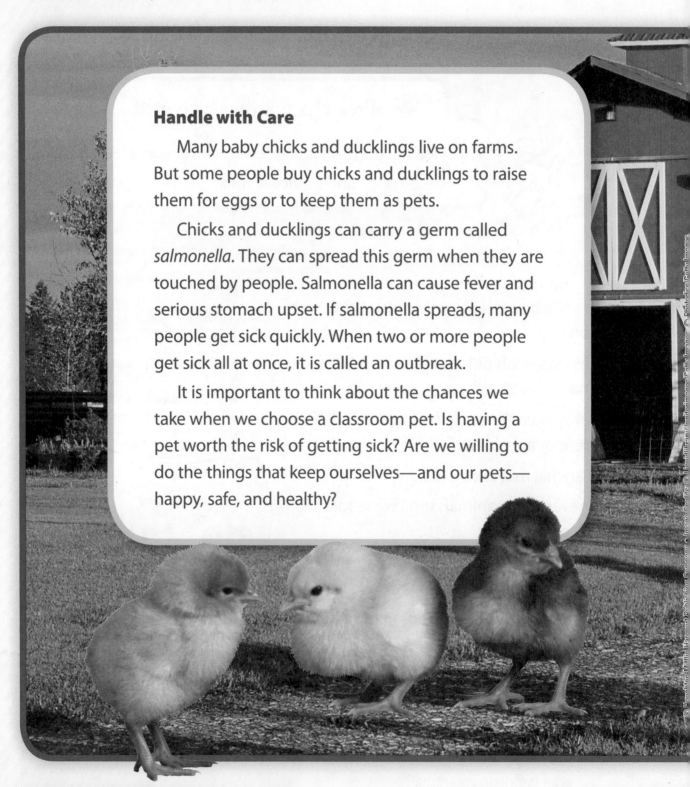

Handle with Care

Many baby chicks and ducklings live on farms. But some people buy chicks and ducklings to raise them for eggs or to keep them as pets.

Chicks and ducklings can carry a germ called *salmonella*. They can spread this germ when they are touched by people. Salmonella can cause fever and serious stomach upset. If salmonella spreads, many people get sick quickly. When two or more people get sick all at once, it is called an outbreak.

It is important to think about the chances we take when we choose a classroom pet. Is having a pet worth the risk of getting sick? Are we willing to do the things that keep ourselves—and our pets— happy, safe, and healthy?

1. Analyze   **2. Practice**   3. Perform

In 10 years, there were 34 salmonella outbreaks linked to live poultry.

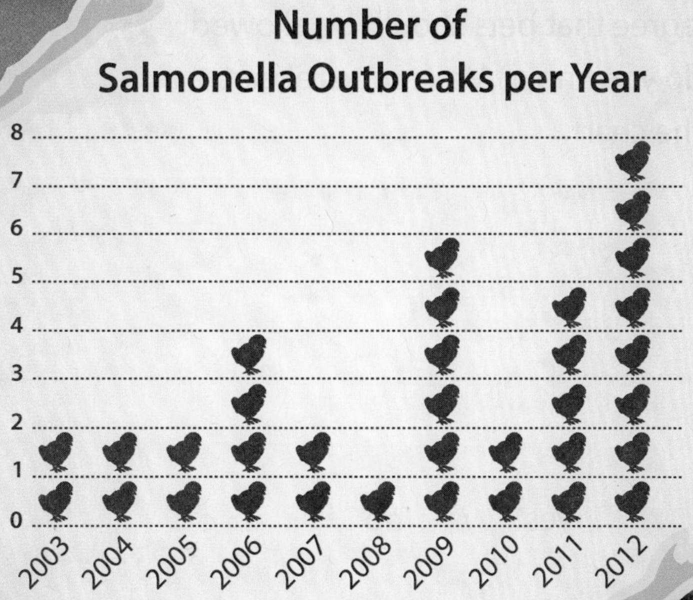

Number of Salmonella Outbreaks per Year

8
7
6
5
4
3
2
1
0

2003 2004 2005 2006 2007 2008 2009 2010 2011 2012

Close Read

What does the data in the graph above add to your understanding of salmonella?

_____

_____

Respond to Questions

These questions will help you analyze the sources you read. Use your notes and refer to the sources in order to answer the questions. Your answers to these questions will help you write your essay.

1 Which source(s) agree that pets should be allowed in school? How do you know? Make notes about your reasons in the chart.

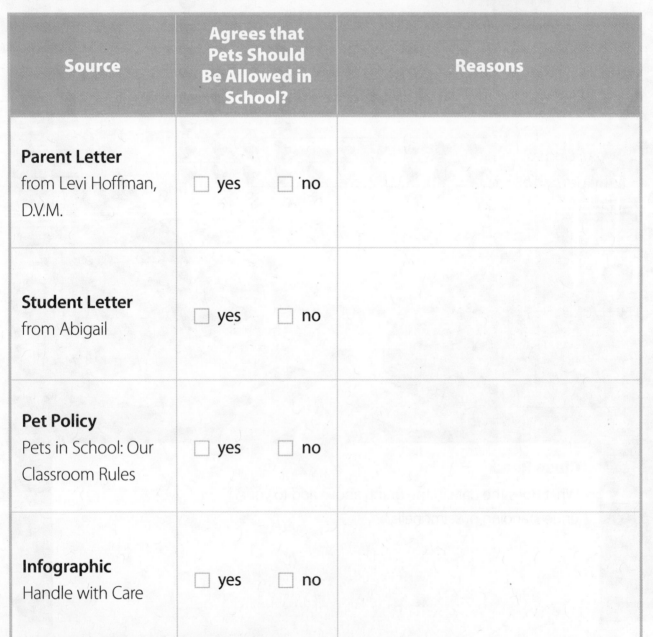

Source	Agrees that Pets Should Be Allowed in School?	Reasons
Parent Letter from Levi Hoffman, D.V.M.	☐ yes ☐ no	
Student Letter from Abigail	☐ yes ☐ no	
Pet Policy Pets in School: Our Classroom Rules	☐ yes ☐ no	
Infographic Handle with Care	☐ yes ☐ no	

2 **Prose Constructed-Response** What is one reason why pets **should** be allowed in school? Cite text evidence in your response.

_____

_____

_____

_____

_____

_____

3 **Prose Constructed-Response** What is one reason why pets **shouldn't** be allowed in school? Cite text evidence in your response.

_____

_____

_____

_____

_____

_____

Planning and Prewriting

Assignment
Write an opinion essay to answer the question: Should pets be allowed in school?

Before you draft your essay, complete some important planning steps.

What's Your Opinion?

You may prefer to plan on a computer.

Think about what you've read and respond below.

Issue: Should pets be allowed in school?

Your position on the issue: ☐ yes ☐ no

Your opinion:

_____

_____

_____

What Are Your Reasons?

Pick three sentences from the sources that helped you form your opinion. Write one sentence in each box below.

Reason	Reason	Reason

1. Analyze   2. Practice   3. Perform

Finalize Your Plan

You know what your opinion is on the issue. Now, it's time to plan the structure of your essay. You will save time and create a more organized, logical essay by planning the structure before you start writing.

Use your responses on pages 22–24 to complete the graphic organizer.

| Introduction | ◀ Grab your reader's attention with an interesting fact or personal story. Identify the issue and your opinion. |

| Reason | Reason | Reason | ◀ State reasons that support your opinion. |

| Opposing Opinion | ◀ Give the opposing opinion and how you will counter it. |

| Concluding Section | ◀ Restate your opinion. |

Draft Your Essay

If you drafted your essay on the computer, you may wish to print it out.

As you write, think about:

▶ **Purpose** *what you want to communicate*

▶ **Clarity** *ideas that are straightforward and understandable*

▶ **Support** *examples from the sources that support your opinion*

▶ **Organization** *the logical structure for your essay*

▶ **Connecting Words** *words that link your ideas*

▶ **Academic Vocabulary** *words used in writing about a particular topic*

Revision Checklist: Self-Evaluation

Use the checklist below to guide your self-evaluation.

Ask Yourself	Make It Better
1. Does your introduction grab the audience's attention?	A great introduction hooks your audience. Ask a question, create a vivid image, or tell a personal story. Make sure you clearly state your opinion up front.
2. Do the reasons support your opinion?	In the body of your essay, give three reasons that support your opinion. Give details or examples to support these reasons.
3. Do connecting words help organize and link ideas in your essay?	Connecting words link ideas together. Use connecting words to signal differences of opinion, explain how two ideas relate, or shift from one paragraph of your essay to the next.
4. Does the essay explain and counter an opposing opinion?	Ask yourself, "What would someone who disagrees with my opinion say about my reasons?" Include an opposing viewpoint and explain how you counter it.
5. Does the last section restate your opinion?	In wrapping up your essay, restate your opinion and provide a summary of the reasons you gave to support your opinion.

1. Analyze **2. Practice** 3. Perform

Revision Checklist: Peer Review

Exchange your essay with a classmate, or read it out loud to your partner. As you read and comment on your partner's essay, focus on organization and evidence. You do not need to agree with your partner's opinion. Help your partner find parts of the draft that need to be revised.

What to Look For	Notes for My Partner
1. Does the introduction grab the audience's attention?	
2. Do the reasons support the stated opinion?	
3. Do connecting words help organize and link ideas in the essay?	
4. Does the essay explain and counter an opposing opinion?	
5. Does the last section restate the opinion?	

Use Connecting Words

Review Your Use of Connecting Words

To make your essay read smoothly and to link your ideas, use connecting words. Connecting words show how two things or ideas are related.

These sentences are choppy and interrupt the flow of ideas:

> She is a good dog. I have taught her to sit, stay, and come.

This sentence is smooth and links both ideas together:

> She is a good dog because I have taught her to sit, stay, and come.

Essay Tips

Use Connecting Words!

Here are some connecting words that you might use when you revise your essay.

although	even though	in addition
because	for example	since
but	for instance	therefore
even if	in order to	while

Edit

Edit your essay to correct spelling, grammar, and punctuation errors.

Which are better: cats or dogs?

You will read:

- **A Letter to the Editor**
  from Henry Regan

- **A Letter to the Editor**
  from Juliette Charles

- **A Fact Sheet**
  Facts About Cats, Data About Dogs

- **A Chart**
  The Internet Loves Dogs

You will write:

- **An Opinion Essay**
  Which are better: cats or dogs?

Source 1: Letter to the Editor

AS YOU READ
Look for reasons that support your opinion, or reasons that make you change your opinion about this question: Which are better: cats or dogs?

Notes

Springfield Weekly ★ June 21

Letters

Dear Editor,

I'm writing today because I disagree with the results of the poll you included in last week's paper. Your poll showed that most readers like cats better than dogs. But I do not think cats make the best pets, and I'll tell you why.

First of all, a dog is known as "man's best friend." We do not call cats anyone's friend. Cats claw people, and they meow for no reason. My dog
10 Shelby only barks when she has to go outside, or when I tell her to "speak."

It's easy to train a dog because a dog wants to please its owner. Cats don't want to please humans. They do not run up to greet you when you come in the door. You can't train a cat.

I love how caring my dog is. Shelby loves to have her ears scratched and her belly rubbed. She loves to be brushed, too. If I tried to rub a cat's belly, I'd get clawed up!

1. Analyze   2. Practice   3. Perform

20   Shelby goes with me everywhere. She can travel in the car, she can go to the park, and she can swim in the lake. You can't bring a cat anywhere without a carrier!

Dogs are also better pets because they take care of us. I walk Shelby every day, so she and I get exercise at the same time. People who own cats don't have to leave the house to take care

30   of their pets! I enjoy having a pet that makes me take care of myself.

I don't know how so many people voted for cats as better pets than dogs, but I'll stick to dogs.

Sincerely,

Henry Regan

Close Read

What is one reason Henry prefers dogs to cats?

Source 2: Letter to the Editor

AS YOU READ

Pay attention to the information in the letter to the editor. Write down comments or questions in the side margins.

Notes

Springfield Weekly ★ June 21

Letters

Dear Editor,

Thank you for the poll you ran last week. I knew that more people liked cats than dogs! I am a cat owner, and I love my cat, Rascal.

Rascal loves to cuddle. Every day when I wake up, he snuggles up close to me. He purrs and purrs! He likes it when I pat him first thing in the morning, and it makes us both feel relaxed and happy.

When I have friends over to visit, Rascal hangs
10 out in a different room. He is shy around new people. I never have to worry that he'll jump on my friends, or bark at them.

My friends who own dogs have to get up early on the weekends to walk their dogs. They have to go outside in bad weather, or when they don't feel well, because dogs need to go outside many times a day. Cats don't need to be walked! Rascal is an indoor cat. I don't have to take him out, and I can leave a bowl of food out for him all day long. You
20 have to feed dogs at a specific time of day.

If I want to go away for a weekend, I can leave out food for Rascal and send a friend to check in on him once. If I had a dog, someone would have to stay at my house, or I would have to send my dog to stay with a friend. Dogs need a lot more attention than cats do.

30 Cats clean themselves, which is why they smell better than dogs. I never have to scrub Rascal in the bathtub! That's a task the dog owners can keep.

I wouldn't trade Rascal for a dog. He may like to spend time on his own, but so do I. Thank you for proving that people think cats are better than dogs!

Sincerely,

Juliette Charles

Close Read

What is one reason Juliette prefers cats to dogs?

Source 3: Fact Sheet

Facts About Cats

- Cats have been companions to humans for 8,000 years!

- Cats sleep about 13–14 hours a day.

- A cat's instincts let it turn itself around in mid-fall and land on its feet.

- Cats have claws that help them climb tall objects and hold onto prey.

- Cats are very quick. They chase and sometimes catch animals that move fast, such as mice.

- Cats keep homes bug-free. Chasing insects is a fun game for them!

Amazing Cats!

- A cat named Scarlett saved all five of her kittens from a burning abandoned garage in New York. She was badly burned from saving them all. "The Scarlett Award for Animal Heroism" is named after Scarlett. It is given to animals that help humans or other animals.

- Tara the cat saved a four year-old boy in California. She chased away an attacking dog that was dragging the boy off.

Data About Dogs

- Dogs have been companions to humans for over 10,000 years!

- Dogs have sensitive noses. Some can smell more than 10,000 times better than humans!

- Think you have great hearing? Think again! Dogs can hear high-pitched sounds that humans cannot hear.

- Service dogs help people do things they may not be able to do for themselves. Seeing-eye dogs help people who are blind.

- Dogs can be taught new tricks at any age.

Amazing Dogs!

- Barry the Saint Bernard was a rescue dog in Switzerland in the early 1800's. He looked for travelers who had been buried in snow. He saved more than 40 human lives.

- 11-year-old Austin was saved by his dog Angel when he was attacked by a cougar near Vancouver, Canada. Angel jumped in front of Austin, saving him from the cougar. Angel had some injuries, but she soon recovered.

Discuss and Decide

According to the fact sheet, what is one way that cats are different from dogs?

The Internet Loves Dogs

I'm Theo, and I love all kinds of animals. I like cats and I like dogs, too. So when my friend Nadine asked me, "Which are better, cats or dogs?" I didn't know how to answer! That's when we went online to find out what the Internet has to say. If you look up these search terms today, what numbers do you get?

meow!

woof!

Google	search term: **cats are better than dogs** about **39.8 million**	search term: **dogs are better than cats** about **40.1 million**
YouTube	search term: **cat** or **cats** about **37.4 million**	search term: **dog** or **dogs** about **36.4 million**
Facebook	"likes" for: **cats** about **2.6 million**	"likes" for: **dogs** about **8.7 million**
Instagram	tagged: **#cat** or **#cats** about **47 million**	tagged: **#dog** or **#dogs** about **46 million**

Discuss and Decide

What details suggest that dogs are more popular than cats?

1. Analyze   2. Practice   3. Perform

Respond to Questions

These questions will help you think about the sources you've read. Use your notes and refer to the sources to answer the questions. Your answers to these questions will help you write your essay.

1 Which of the following statements is a fact?

   a. "... they meow for no reason." (Source 1)

   b. "Dogs are also better pets ..." (Source 1)

   c. "You have to feed dogs at a specific time of day." (Source 2)

   d. "Cats have claws that help them climb tall objects and hold onto prey." (Source 3)

2 According to Source 1, why are dogs better than cats?

   a. They encourage people to take care of themselves.

   b. They are clean.

   c. They are easy to care for.

   d. They have to travel in carriers.

3 Which sentence best supports your answer to Question 2?

   a. "My dog Shelby only barks when she has to go outside, or when I tell her to to 'speak.'"

   b. "You can't bring a cat anywhere without a carrier!"

   c. "Dogs are also better pets because they take care of us."

   d. "People who own cats don't have to leave the house to take care of their pets!"

4 Which sentence best supports the idea that cats are brave?

    a. "Cats clean themselves, which is why they smell better than dogs." (Source 2)

    b. "Their claws help them climb tall objects and hold onto prey." (Source 3)

    c. "Scarlett saved all five of her kittens from a burning abandoned garage in New York." (Source 3)

    d. Google has about 535 million cat links. (Source 4)

5 Which source(s) agree that cats are better? Which source(s) agree that dogs are better? How do you know? Make notes about your reasons in the chart.

Source	Which are better?		Reasons
Letter to the Editor from Henry Regan	☐ cats	☐ dogs	
Letter to the Editor from Juliette Charles	☐ cats	☐ dogs	
Fact Sheet Facts About Cats Data About Dogs	☐ cats	☐ dogs	
Chart The Internet Loves Dogs	☐ cats	☐ dogs	

6 **Prose-Constructed Response** What information in Source 3 can support the writer's opinion in Source 1? Explain. Cite evidence from the text in your response.

_____

_____

Write the Essay

Read the assignment.

Plan

Use the graphic organizer to help you outline the structure of your opinion essay.

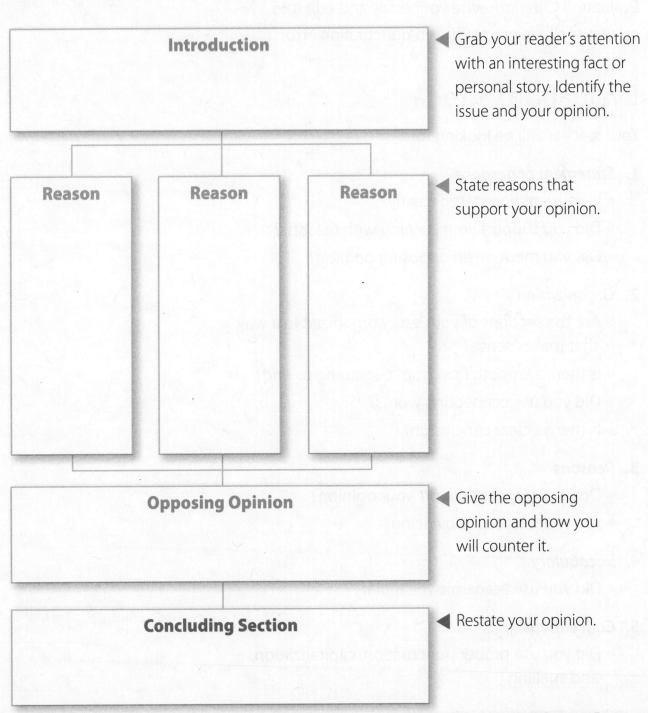

Introduction

◄ Grab your reader's attention with an interesting fact or personal story. Identify the issue and your opinion.

Reason   **Reason**   **Reason**

◄ State reasons that support your opinion.

Opposing Opinion

◄ Give the opposing opinion and how you will counter it.

Concluding Section

◄ Restate your opinion.

Draft

Use your notes and completed graphic organizer to write a first draft of your opinion essay.

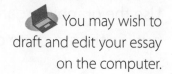

Revise and Edit

Look back over your essay and compare it to the Evaluation Criteria. Revise your essay and edit it to correct spelling, grammar, and punctuation errors.

You may wish to draft and edit your essay on the computer.

Evaluation Criteria

Your teacher will be looking for:

1. *Statement of purpose*
- Is your opinion stated clearly?
- Did you support your opinion with reasons?
- Did you mention an opposing opinion?

2. *Organization*
- Are the sections of your essay organized in a way that makes sense?
- Is there a smooth flow from beginning to end?
- Did you use connecting words?
- Is there a clear conclusion?

3. *Reasons*
- Do your reasons support your opinion?
- Are your reasons convincing?

4. *Vocabulary*
- Did you use academic vocabulary?

5. *Conventions*
- Did you use proper punctuation, capitalization, and spelling?

250 Years Ago

Unit 2
Informative Essay

Step 1

Analyze the Model

Evaluate an informative essay about American Indian homes and food.

Step 2

Practice the Task

Write an informative essay about transportation in colonial America.

Step 3

Perform the Task

Write an informative essay about the everyday life of colonial children.

An informative essay gives facts about a topic. The purpose of the essay is to present and explain true information. An informative essay usually discusses real events, real people, and real places. Examples of informative writing include biographies, newspaper articles, speeches, and true-life adventure stories.

The sources in this unit explain what life was like for people in America 250 years ago. You will read about the American Indians who were native to the land and the colonists who had come to America over time. The information is factual.

IN THIS UNIT, you will evaluate the way writers organized their informative essays and analyze information from nonfiction articles, maps, and photographs. Then you will use what you have learned to write informative essays of your own.

How did American Indians' surroundings affect the way they lived?

You will read:

- **A Food Magazine Column**
  A Monthly History of American Food

- **An Informational Article**
  American Indian Homes

You will analyze:

- **A Student Model**
  You Are Where You Live

Source 1: Food Magazine Column

Mrs. Novak's student, Seiji Ando, used two sources for an essay answering the question "How did American Indians' surroundings affect the way they lived?" As you read each source, make notes in the side columns. Underline helpful information.

Notes

A Monthly History of American Food

By Noura Nazari

This month, we'll look at the foods that American Indians ate 250 years ago.

The main crops grown by American Indians were corn, beans, and squash. The beans were planted next to the corn, and as they grew they climbed up the tall corn stalks. The more the beans grew, the more they improved the soil, helping the corn to grow, too. Between rows of corn and beans, the people planted squash. The large squash leaves stopped weeds from growing. They also shaded the shallow roots of the corn plants and helped keep the ground damp. This allowed the corn and beans to grow more. The arrangement was perfect, and the three crops together are known as the "three sisters."

1. Analyze   2. Practice   3. Perform

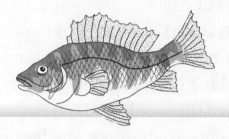

In the Eastern Woodlands, summers were warm and wet. The three sisters grew easily. Woodlands tribes also hunted animals that lived in the woods, and they caught fish and shellfish in the rivers and the ocean.

The climate of the Southwest is dry. But there is some summer rain, and winter snow in the mountains melts. It feeds rivers, streams, and springs. The Pueblo Indians of the Southwest controlled the water by digging ditches across the land, so they too could grow the three sisters. Pueblo tribes also raised sheep and goats.

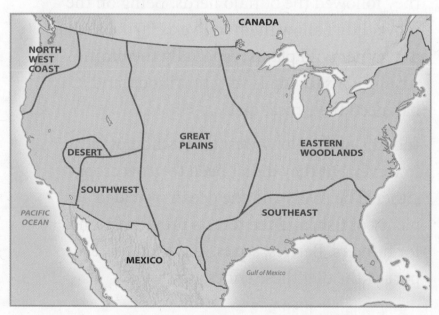

Some areas of America are even drier than the Southwest. Desert Indians lived in places where there were not many animals to hunt and the land didn't support crops. These Indians hunted what they could and traveled around gathering nuts, seeds, roots, and berries.

Plains Indians, too, did not grow many crops. Their food came from the buffalo. There were tens of millions of these animals migrating through the Great Plains, in herds numbering in the hundreds of thousands. The Plains Indians also hunted elk, deer, and antelope, but they followed the buffalo herds. Being on the move didn't allow them to live as farmers. They did gather wild plants, especially the prairie turnip. This turnip is very nutritious, and it balanced their meat diet.

Indians of the Northwest Coast did not have to travel, but they didn't need to grow crops either. The rivers and the ocean provided plenty of fish, and the forests provided game for hunters. Berries, seeds, and roots were also part of the diet these tribes ate.

Here's an easy recipe for Three Sisters Succotash. You'll need:

- 1 cup corn kernels
- 2 summer squash, chopped
- 2 zucchini, chopped
- 1 cup cooked lima beans
- 1 tablespoon bear grease (you can use olive oil)
- sage powder, salt, and pepper to taste

Heat the oil in a large skillet. Add the squash and cook for about 3 minutes. Stir often. Then add the corn and cook for another 3 minutes, stirring. Finally, add the lima beans and cook until they are hot. Add a pinch of salt, pepper, and sage powder. Some people like to add tomatoes, too.

Discuss and Decide

Explain the differences between what the Desert Indians and the Plains Indians ate.

American Indian Homes

The kinds of homes that American Indians lived in 250 years ago depended on several things. These included the local weather, the materials that were available, and whether or not the people stayed in the same place all year round.

American Indians of the Great Plains were nomads. They traveled from place to place as they hunted buffalo. These people lived in teepees, built with long poles covered with buffalo hide. Teepees were easy to set up and to move.

In the Southwest, American Indians built pueblos out of adobe, a mixture of clay and straw. Pueblos were like villages of apartment houses. Each family lived in an apartment all year round. The buildings were similar to older pueblos that had been built into the sides of cliffs.

In northern parts of the Southeast, American Indians built homes with wattle and daub. These materials, used for the walls, are thin branches and clay. The branches were woven together and then covered with clay. The roof of the house was thatch, made of bundles of dried grasses.

In the Eastern Woodlands, American Indians lived in longhouses. They were usually about 180 feet long, and each was home to many families of the same clan. Longhouses were built with sheets of bark covering a wooden frame, and had openings in the roof to let smoke from fires escape.

American Indians who lived near the coast in the Northwest built plank houses. These were made with long planks of cedar from the surrounding forests. Each house could be home to a few families. It took time and effort to build these large homes, but the people lived in them all year long.

The Inuit of the far North built igloos from blocks of snow. Strange as it seems, the inside of an igloo can be quite warm. Small igloos were built for shelter on hunting trips, while the largest igloos had a number of rooms and could be winter homes for up to 20 people. In summer months, the Inuit made tents of animal skins.

Close Read

What are two reasons the Plains Indians chose to live in teepees?

Analyze a Student Model

Seiji wrote an essay that answered the question: "How did American Indians' surroundings affect the way they lived?" The red notes are the comments that his teacher, Mrs. Novak, wrote.

Seiji Ando

April 7

You Are  Where You Live

Great way to introduce the idea that surroundings affect the way people live.

People need shelter and they need food. People who lived 250 years ago built homes that were suited to their surroundings. They ate the kinds of food that their surroundings could provide.

American Indian tribes that moved around a lot needed homes they could carry with them. Plains Indians followed migrating buffalo herds. The buffalo was their main food. So they made homes they could move easily. Their teepees were covered with buffalo hides, too.

You cited details from both sources here. Good thinking!

Other American Indians stayed in one place and grew crops. In the Eastern Woodlands, the main crops were corn, beans, and squash. The people also hunted animals and caught fish.

1. Analyze 2. Practice 3. Perform

The houses they built were called longhouses. They used wood and bark from the trees in the forest.

In the Southwest, Pueblo Indians also grew crops of corn, beans, and squash. They could stay in the same place all the time. They built pueblos of clay and straw. A pueblo is a bit like an apartment building.

The Northwest Coast had the ocean and rivers that were full of fish. The forests had game. There were berries, seeds, and roots. The people who lived there had food all year long and didn't need to grow crops. They built plank houses with cedar wood from the forests.

Were the ocean and rivers really "full" of fish? Maybe use another word.

American Indian homes were built with the materials that were available. They had to match their owners' way of life. The food the Indians ate was from their surroundings.

Nice wrap-up.

Discuss and Decide

Find two examples where Seiji included details from both sources in a single paragraph.

Organizing an Informative Essay

You can organize an informative essay in various ways. In the student model "You Are Where You Live," Seiji used cause and effect. He began the essay with an overall look at the causes and effects in American Indians' lives. Then he gave specific examples of each cause and effect in the paragraphs that follow. In the last paragraph, Seiji sums up his ideas.

Complete the chart below with examples from Seiji's essay.

Introduction

Cause: People need shelter and food.

Effect: American Indians built homes suited to their surroundings and ate food their surroundings could provide.

◀ The opening paragraph states what causes and effects will be in the essay.

Cause and Effect

◀ The following paragraphs give details and examples of causes and effects.

Cause and Effect

Cause and Effect

Conclusion

◀ The last paragraph sums up the causes and effects in the essay. You might add your own insights on the topic.

How did colonists travel in America?

You will read:

- **A Magazine Article**
  Travel in 18th-Century America

- **Journal Excerpts**
  Remarks Made by James Birket in His Voyage to North America

You will write:

- **An Informative Essay**
  How did colonists travel in America?

AS YOU READ You will be writing an informative essay that explains how colonists traveled in America. As you read the article, underline information that may be helpful.

Travel in 18th-Century America

by Diana Dubois

When you travel today, you get in a car, ride on a bus, or maybe fly in a plane. But 250 years ago, none of these ways of traveling existed. Even trains wouldn't appear for about another 60 years. Getting around wasn't easy. There weren't many good roads or bridges. People didn't always have good directions, so it was easy to get lost. But people, animals, goods, and letters still managed to move. Here's how they did it.

On Foot

Walking was the most common way to get around. Everyone did a lot of walking. You might be poor or you might be rich, but you would still walk. Farmers, lawyers, landowners, and governors all walked. Many of the roads they took between towns were Indian trails that had been widened. These roads presented all sorts of dangers such as mud, rocks, uneven ground, and fallen trees. Records from the time talk about how common injuries were, even on good roads or highways.

On Horseback

Horses were a quicker way to get around if you had the money. A horse could cost as little as five pounds (about $1,000 today). Most horses were more expensive. James Birket, a traveler through the colonies, bought his horse for 160 pounds (over $30,000 today). Even poor colonists would buy a horse and saddle as soon as they could afford them. It was a common sight to see a farmer riding his horse with his wife sitting behind him on a cushion. Of course, horses had to cross the same rough countryside and travel along the same bumpy roads as people who traveled on foot.

By Carriage

Wealthy travelers could travel longer distances in greater comfort. For these long journeys, they would travel by stagecoach, a covered carriage pulled by horses. It was called a stagecoach because the trip was made in stages. At each stop, horses were allowed to rest and new horses were switched in to pull the coach.

Horses also pulled other kinds of carriages for shorter distances. One common carriage was the one-horse shay, which had two wheels

and seated two people. It could be covered or uncovered. There was also the curricle, a two-wheeled carriage which was pulled by two horses of equal size. Shays and curricles were mostly used for pleasure rides and short trips.

Conestoga wagons (from Conestoga, Pennsylvania) were not used for pleasure or short trips. They carried common goods like flour, wheat, produce, spices, tea, and clothing to far-off towns to sell. Families also used them when they packed up and moved to a new place. These wagons were huge—the average size was usually sixteen feet long, four feet wide, and four feet deep. Some could carry as much as 8 tons! They had canvas covers to protect the goods inside from bad weather. Many Conestoga wagons made the trip from Philadelphia to North Carolina on the Great Wagon Road.

Whatever kind of horse-drawn carriage you rode in, the trip was probably not very comfortable. Most carriages didn't have springs, so you could feel every bump in the very bumpy roads. They would often get stuck in mud, and passengers would have to help push them out. Passengers also had to get up hours before sunrise and then ride as much as 18 hours in a day. Even so, a trip from Boston to New York could easily take six days!

By Boat

Water travel was often the easiest and fastest way to go, because the roads were so bad. Of course, you could only travel where there was water. For moving up and down rivers and other smaller bodies of water, a small sailboat called a sloop was common. Canoes, rafts, and flatboats were also used for shorter trips and to transport wood, food, and furs. Larger boats sailed up and down the east coast of America, and huge ships crossed the Atlantic Ocean carrying people and goods between America and Europe.

Travel in the colonies depended on the power of the wind, water, animals, or your own two feet. Until the introduction of steam power in the early 1800s, travel in America remained much as it had for hundreds of years—slow.

Close Read

List two reasons why traveling in the 18th century was difficult. Cite text evidence in your response.

_____

_____

_____

_____

Source 2: Journal Excerpts

AS YOU READ Analyze the journal entries. Continue to write notes and underline information that will help you write your essay.

Remarks Made by James Birket in His Voyage to North America

In 1750, James Birket made a journey through the American colonies. He kept a journal of some of his thoughts about his travels. Here are a few of his journal entries.

* * *

September 3, 1750 *(Ipswich, Massachusetts)*

They have some coasting vessels that come below the town where they unload and load cargo. We crossed this river at the end of the town by a wooden bridge. From Ipswich to Beverley Ferry is ten miles, and it is one mile on the other side to Salem. This last part is excellent road and very even. Smooth and hard gravel.

September 4, 1750 *(Salem, Massachusetts)*

I drove the horse and carriage in two and a half hours from Salem to the ferry, fifteen miles at least. We got over the ferry by 11 o'clock. . . . In the evening I went with Henry Vassels in his carriage. It is eight miles the land way, but over the Charlestown ferry it is only four miles.

October 3, 1750 *(Newport, Rhode Island)*

We took a boat from the point and in about two hours landed on Conanicut Island. It is three miles away, but the wind blew very strongly against us. We crossed the island to the next ferry, but it blew so hard we could not get over. We had to dine with an ill-natured man at the ferry house. After dinner we got the ferry for three miles, taking two hours. The wind continued to blow hard against us. We traveled five miles to Tower Hill on a very bad stony road . . . this country has a lot of stones.

October 5, 1750 *(Charlestown, Rhode Island)*

We set out pretty early. After riding a mile we left the Indian wigwams on our left and their king's palace on our right. . . . We rode twenty-one miles to the banks of the river Thames. Then we crossed the river by the ferry boat where it is about a mile over. We stayed with Captain Bradocks, who used to be a sea captain. He behaved with great politeness and good manners to his guests when compared with the rude lazy loafers of this part of the world.

October 8, 1750 *(New London, Connecticut)*

We had a very stony road for six miles to the rope ferry. We got over very well. It is so narrow that a rope is stretched across for the safety of travelers, as the tide runs here with great violence.

1. Analyze   2. Practice   3. Perform

October 11, 1750 *(Norwalk, Connecticut)*

We had very heavy rain and it was quite dark. It was the most unbearably bad road. We stayed with an unnatural old fellow who did not want to give us lodging. His one-eyed wife was little better. She wanted her barefooted son to share with one of us. We all refused. Where he went I do not know and neither do I care.

Discuss and Decide
What advantages and disadvantages were there to taking a ferry rather than riding?

Respond to Questions

These questions will help you examine the sources you read. Use your notes and refer to the sources in order to answer the questions. Your answers to these questions will help you write your essay.

1 Which sentence from Source 1 best describes the experience of riding in a carriage?

   a. "They carried common goods . . . to far-off towns to sell."

   b. "Conestoga wagons . . . were not used for pleasure or short trips."

   c. "Most carriages didn't have springs, so you could feel every bump in the very bumpy roads."

   d. "Families also used them when they packed up and moved to a new place."

2 What is the meaning of *sloop* as it is used in Source 1?

   a. river

   b. boat

   c. common

   d. fur

3 What claim can you make based on the information in Source 2?

   a. All of the roads in America were unbearably bad.

   b. The weather could affect how long a journey took.

   c. The only way to cross a river was by ferry.

   d. A good horse could carry a rider 50 miles in a day.

4 From Birket's accounts, what can you tell about the colonies of Massachusetts, Rhode Island, and Connecticut?

   a. The weather was usually bad.

   b. There were many American Indians living there.

   c. There were a lot of rivers there.

   d. Most people there traveled by horse.

5 **Prose Constructed-Response** What is the main idea of the section labeled "On Horseback" in Source 1? Cite text evidence in your response.

_____

_____

_____

_____

6 **Prose Constructed-Response** How does the information in both sources show that traveling on roads in colonial America was difficult? Cite text evidence in your response.

_____

_____

_____

_____

_____

Planning and Prewriting

When you write an informative essay, first think about how you will organize it. Since the essay question asks for several details related to travel, you could write a main-idea-and-details essay. Think about the main idea that covers all the important information you read about how colonists traveled.

Assignment

Write an informative essay to answer the question: How did colonists travel in America?

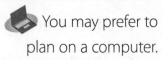 You may prefer to plan on a computer.

Collect Information

Only include information from a source if it is directly related to the topic you're covering. Extra information might make your informative essay confusing.

Complete the chart with information you'll use from each source.

Source	Evidence from Source	Details
Magazine Article Travel in 18th-Century America		
Journal Excerpts Remarks Made by James Birket in His Voyage to North America		

© Houghton Mifflin Harcourt Publishing Company

Finalize Your Plan

Use your responses and notes from previous pages to make a plan for your essay.

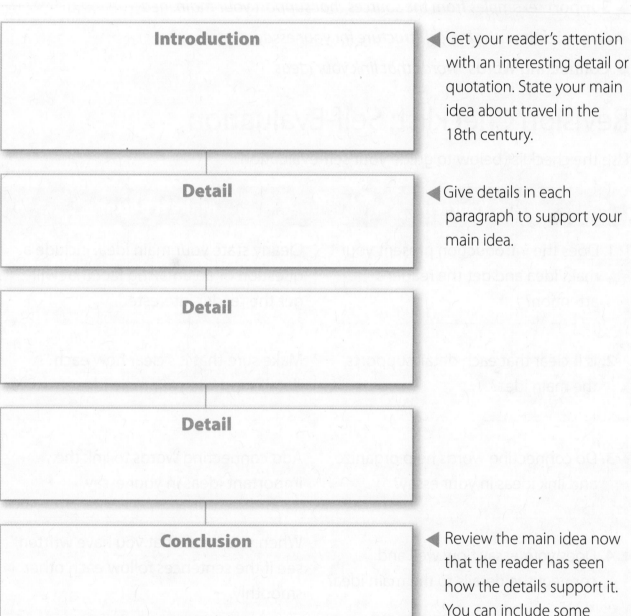

Introduction

◀ Get your reader's attention with an interesting detail or quotation. State your main idea about travel in the 18th century.

Detail

◀ Give details in each paragraph to support your main idea.

Detail

Detail

Conclusion

◀ Review the main idea now that the reader has seen how the details support it. You can include some thoughts of your own about the topic.

Draft Your Essay

If you drafted your essay on the computer, you may wish to print it out.

As you write, think about:

▶ **Purpose** *to use sources for a main idea-and-details essay*

▶ **Clarity** *straightforward writing that is easy to understand*

▶ **Support** *examples from the sources that support your main idea*

▶ **Organization** *the logical structure for your essay*

▶ **Connecting Words** *words that link your ideas*

Revision Checklist: Self-Evaluation

Use the checklist below to guide your self-evaluation.

Ask Yourself	Make It Better
1. Does the introduction present your main idea and get the reader's attention?	Clearly state your main idea. Include a question or an amazing fact that will get the reader interested.
2. Is it clear that each detail supports the main idea?	Make sure that it's clear how each detail supports your main idea.
3. Do connecting words help organize and link ideas in your essay?	Add connecting words to link the important ideas in your essay.
4. Does your essay flow well and connect the details to the main idea?	When you read what you have written, see if the sentences follow each other smoothly.
5. Does the conclusion restate the main idea based on the support from the details?	Make sure your main idea is based on the details in your essay. You can also add an idea of your own about your understanding of the topic.

Revision Checklist: Peer Review

Exchange essays with a classmate. Read your partner's essay, and make comments. Think about how well it describes and explains travel in colonial America.

Help your partner find ways to improve the essay.

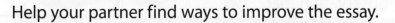

What to Look For	Notes for My Partner
1. Does the introduction present the main idea and get the reader's attention?	
2. Is it clear that each detail supports the main idea?	
3. Do connecting words help organize and link ideas in the essay?	
4. Does the essay flow well and connect the details to the main idea?	
5. Does the conclusion restate the main idea based on the support from the details?	

Revision: Writing an Introduction

You want your audience to read what you have written. So, it's a good idea to capture the reader's attention at the beginning of your essay. One way to do this is to start by presenting an observation that is new to the reader. Make sure your observation is about your main idea.

This introduction gets the reader's attention with an observation about travel.

> It isn't hard to visit your closest relatives if they live only 20 miles away. But if you could go back 250 years, you would find out just how far 20 miles is. Traveling in the 1700s was difficult. There were few roads, which were often little more than tracks. The only power you could use was your own feet, an animal's feet, or the wind.

Attention-Getting Advice

- Tie your main idea to an interesting observation.

- Use a quote that gets the reader to wonder about your topic.

- Present a surprising fact about your topic.

- Write about an exciting event that relates to your topic.

- Ask a question that makes the reader want to know the answer.

Edit

Edit your essay to correct spelling, grammar, and punctuation errors.

What was everyday life like for children in colonial America?

You will read:

- **A Journal Entry**
  Rick's Journal

- **An Informational Article**
  Colonial School Days

- **A Gift Shop Catalog**
  New at the Store!

You will write:

- **An Informative Essay**
  What was everyday life like for children in colonial America?

Source 1: Journal Entry

Rick's Journal

April 16th

Today I went with my mom and dad to the 13 Colonies Museum and Historical Site.

There were lots of kids around my age, but they looked very different. The boys wore buckled shoes, linen shirts, and breeches. Those are pants that go down to
10   just below the knees. Girls wore long dresses and hats. Younger boys and girls wore frocks, which are like dresses with sashes. Some little kids wore tight leather vests called bodices to keep their posture straight. The bodices had strings attached to the shoulders so parents could help the really little kids learn how to walk. I don't think I'd like my mom or dad walking me on a string!

Most kids spent more time working than going to school. One boy was the son of a blacksmith, so he
20   helped his dad make axes, horseshoes, and even swords. Other boys were learning how to make shoes, candles, saddles, and wigs.

Many of the kids I saw were from farming families. They worked from sunrise to sunset everyday. And I thought school was hard! An older boy explained that they had to clear away trees and plow the land to get it ready for planting. Boys would also hunt pigs and deer. Girls spun wool, made clothes, and watched out for their little brothers and sisters. The younger kids would do easier chores like carrying water, husking corn, or gathering eggs.

The kids let me in on a secret. They said they would play games while they worked to make it more fun and to make the job go faster. When they had to carry wood, they would have a contest to see who could carry the most at one time. That seems like an exhausting game!

Anyway, I want to go back there soon.

Close Read

What were some jobs that children on a colonial farm did? Cite text evidence in your response.

_____

_____

Colonial School Days

by Amanda Schultz

School in 18th-century America had little in common with school today. A boy from a rich family might be sent overseas to study in Europe. But if you were a typical child in the city, your first school would be a dame school.

The word "Dame" was used instead of "Mrs." So, a dame school was run by a married woman.
10 It would usually be in the teacher's house. There, children would learn the three Rs: reading, 'riting, and 'rithmetic. There were no gym, music, or science classes. Not even recess! Children didn't go to school as often as they do today. Many children didn't go to school at all. Their families might be too poor to pay for it, or they had to help their parents with work at home.

After finishing dame school at about the age of 10, some boys might continue learning in other
20 schools. But many would become apprentices to their fathers or uncles so they could continue a family business like carpentry or tailoring.

If you grew up in a frontier town, most of your time would be spent working on the family farm. Sometimes you might go to a one-room schoolhouse, which would probably be a log cabin with a dirt floor. Children sat on benches and studied letters and numbers on a "hornbook," a transparent sheet of animal hoof covering printed

30   paper on a board. A day at a frontier school was long. Students would stay for lunch and dinner, too, because many students had to walk or ride a horse many miles to and from the school each day.

So, some children didn't go to school at all. Some went only every now and then, and worked the rest of the time. Some spent their time learning a trade. Whichever it was, a colonial child's day would be long and busy.

Discuss and Decide

What were the main subjects that colonial children studied in school?

NEW at the store!

13 Colonies
Museum and Historical Site

Fun new additions to our museum store!
Just like the toys and games in our exhibits!
Make the past come alive every time you play!

Ring Taw

Ring Taw was a popular marble game in the mid-18th century.

- Draw a large circle (about 7 feet in diameter) on the ground with a piece of chalk.

- Put the 10 small marbles in the center of the circle.

- Give each player one of the larger marbles (called a taw).

- The first player shoots the taw from outside the circle at the marbles in the middle, and keeps any marbles he or she knocks out of the circle. The player continues to shoot until no marbles are knocked out of the circle. Then the next player takes his or her turn.

- The game ends when all the marbles have been knocked out. The player with the most marbles wins!

This set includes 10 small marbles and 2 taws.

Ninepins

You know about tenpin bowling, but here's your chance to try the most popular kind of bowling in colonial America.

- Set the pins up in a diamond shape with the red pin in the center.

- Roll the ball at the pins the way you would in tenpin bowling. If you knock all the pins down, you get 9 points, but if you leave only the center red pin standing, you get 12 points.

- Each player gets to roll twice. If a player can't knock all the pins down in two tries, the next bowler on the team tries to knock down the remaining pins.

- The highest team score wins!

This set includes 8 plain pins, one red pin, and a ball.

Cornhusk Dolls

In the mid-1700s, there were no factories to make the kinds of toys and dolls you might play with today. Children often made dolls out of cornhusks or other things they might find around their homes and farms.

Buy a pre-made doll or try making one yourself with our do-it-yourself kits!

17 Games From the 1700s

Popular games from 250 years ago!

Pick up this book and learn about all sorts of popular games from 250 years ago!

17 Games from the 1700s

This book is a collection of the most popular games colonial children played. It includes old favorites like tag and hopscotch. But there are many games you probably don't know, like thread the needle, cat's cradle, and huzzlecap.

- In the game Shuffling the Brogue, children form a circle and select one person to stand in the center. That person is blindfolded.

- The children in the circle pass a small object around. The child in the center tries to guess who has the object.

- If the guess is right, the person caught with the object takes the place of the child in the center.

Discuss and Decide

What are some differences between dolls of today and the dolls of 250 years ago?

Respond to Questions

The following questions will help you think about the sources you've read. Use your notes and refer to the sources as you answer the questions. Your answers will help you write the essay.

1 What is the best meaning for the word *apprentice* as it is used in Source 2?

   a. a family member

   b. a kind of school

   c. someone who learns a business from a more experienced person

   d. someone who goes to a dame school

2 What was the main reason that many children in the colonies didn't go to school very often?

   a. They had to help their families with work.

   b. They had too many games to play.

   c. They were sent to Europe.

   d. Schools were too far away.

3 Which of the following is a claim you could make based on the information in the sources?

   a. Children were too busy to ever play games.

   b. Frocks were only worn by little girls.

   c. Colonial kids bought toys the same way kids do today.

   d. Some of the games colonial kids played are still around today.

④ Which statement best describes what children learned at a colonial school?

a. "There, children would learn the three Rs: reading, 'riting, and 'rithmetic."

b. "If you grew up in a frontier town, most of your time would be spent working on the family farm."

c. "A day at a frontier school was long."

d. " . . . a dame school was run by a married woman."

⑤ **Prose Constructed-Response** What did boys do after finishing dame school? Cite details from Source 2 in your response.

_____

_____

_____

_____

⑥ **Prose Constructed-Response** Review the three sources. Which source gives you the best understanding of what colonial kids did for fun? Cite text evidence in your response.

_____

_____

_____

_____

Write the Essay

Read the assignment.

Plan

Use the graphic organizer to help you outline the structure of your informative essay.

Assignment

You have read about the experiences of children 250 years ago. Write an informative essay explaining what their everyday lives were like. Organize your essay using main idea and details. Cite text evidence from what you have read.

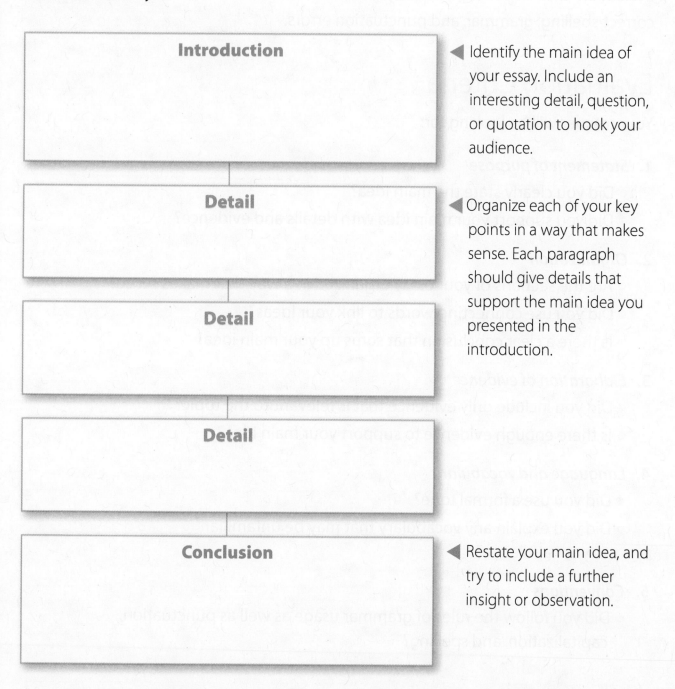

Introduction

◀ Identify the main idea of your essay. Include an interesting detail, question, or quotation to hook your audience.

Detail

◀ Organize each of your key points in a way that makes sense. Each paragraph should give details that support the main idea you presented in the introduction.

Detail

Detail

Conclusion

◀ Restate your main idea, and try to include a further insight or observation.

Draft

Use your notes and completed graphic organizer
to write a first draft of your opinion essay.

Revise and Edit

Look back over your essay and compare it to the
Evaluation Criteria. Revise your essay and edit it to
correct spelling, grammar, and punctuation errors.

You may wish to
draft and edit your essay
on the computer.

Evaluation Criteria

Your teacher will be looking for:

1. **Statement of purpose**
   - Did you clearly state the main idea?
   - Did you support your main idea with details and evidence?

2. **Organization**
   - Are the sections of your essay organized in a way that makes sense?
   - Did you use connecting words to link your ideas?
   - Is there a clear conclusion that sums up your main idea?

3. **Elaboration of evidence**
   - Did you include only evidence that is relevant to the topic?
   - Is there enough evidence to support your main idea?

4. **Language and vocabulary**
   - Did you use a formal tone?
   - Did you explain any vocabulary that may be unfamiliar
     to your audience?

5. **Conventions**
   - Did you follow the rules of grammar usage as well as punctuation,
     capitalization, and spelling?

Animal Tricksters

Response to Literature

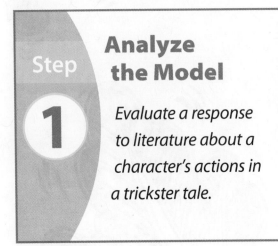

Step 1

Analyze the Model

Evaluate a response to literature about a character's actions in a trickster tale.

Step 2

Practice the Task

Write a response to a fable, explaining how a trickster gets what he wants.

Step 3

Perform the Task

Write a response to a trickster tale, describing the character traits of a trickster.

Stories about animal tricksters have been passed from generation to generation by storytellers. While these stories are entertaining, they also teach lessons about life. One tale may show that people should be kind to others. Another may make it clear that there are consequences to boasting.

The selections in this unit are animal trickster stories from different cultures. Like other folk tales, fables, and trickster tales, these stories may appear in different forms all over the world. The characters may be different, but the message stays the same.

IN THIS UNIT, you will evaluate a student's response to the African trickster tale "Anansi and the Pot of Beans." Then you will read the Greek fable "The Fox and the Crow" and write a response to it. Finally, you will read the American Indian trickster tale "Turtle Races with Beaver" and write a response to it.

How do a character's actions drive the events of a story?

You will read:

- **An African Trickster Tale**

  Anansi and the Pot of Beans

You will analyze:

- **A Student Model**

  Blame It on the Beans

Source: African Trickster Tale

Mr. Cummings' student, Molly Ryan, used this trickster tale as the source for her essay, "Blame It on the Beans." As you read, make notes in the side columns. Underline information that you find useful.

Notes

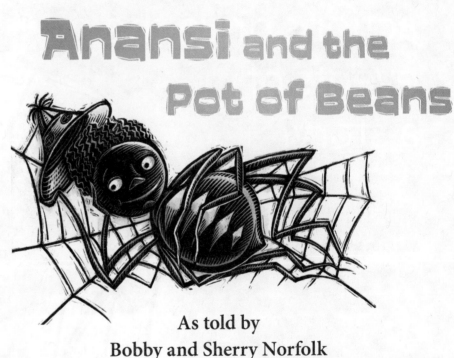

Anansi and the Pot of Beans

As told by Bobby and Sherry Norfolk

Early one morning, Anansi Spider went to help Grandma Spider. He knocked on her door.

"Grandson!" Grandma said as she greeted him with a hug.

Anansi blushed, "Hello, Grandma."

"Grandma Spider," said Anansi. "Do you have any work for me today?"

"Sure," said Grandma Spider. "I want you to plant some beans in my garden."

10   Grandma showed Anansi what she wanted done in the garden. Then she went back into the house to fix some lunch.

    Anansi dropped beans into small holes in the ground. The sun grew warm, and then hot. By noon, Anansi was limp with the heat.

    "It's hot and I'm getting thirsty." Anansi pulled the brim of his hat
20 down to shield his face from the sun.

Notes

Discuss and Decide

What does Grandma Spider ask Anansi to do?

Grandma Spider came to the porch with a large pitcher of fresh lemonade and called to him, "Anansi! Here is a cool drink for you."

"Thank you, Grandma," he said as he drank the cold, sweet lemonade. "I'm making your favorite meal," said Grandma. "I'm cooking spicy beans! They'll be ready soon for our lunch."

"I love your spicy beans!" said Anansi. He
30 finished his lemonade and went back to his work. Grandma Spider returned to the kitchen.

Grandma Spider looked for her bean spices, but the tins were empty. She called, "Anansi! I need spices. I must go to the market. Will you be okay?"

"Sure, Grandma," he answered, "I'll be here in the garden."

"Stay away from that pot of beans! The beans are too hot and the pot

40 is too heavy—you understand me, Anansi?"

"Yes, Ma'am, I understand you. I won't go near that pot of beans!"

The smell of yummy beans rose from the pot and drifted out the window right into Anansi's nose.

"Mmmmmmm!" Anansi's nose twitched and his mouth began to water.

50 He followed the smell into the kitchen until he was standing at the stove with the pot of beans right under his nose.

"Grandma said not to go near these beans. I'd better leave." He turned to go back to the garden, but the smell pulled at him.

"I'm sure it's all right just to SMELL the beans!" he said to himself. Anansi lifted the lid and hot steam filled the air.

"Ahhhhhh!" Anansi took a deep breath of
60 the steam. "I'm sure it's all right to just taste the beans. Grandma won't have to know."

Discuss and Decide

What do Anansi's actions tell you about his character?

He dipped Grandma Spider's big spoon into the pot.

Anansi blew on the hot beans and tasted them. "AHHHH . . ." He spooned up some more . . . sluuuurp . . . he spooned and blew . . . sluuurp . . . he spooned and blew and slurped up spoonful after spoonful of beans.

"Grandma will come back soon. I don't want to get caught!" Anansi thought, "I know! I'll put the beans in my hat and Grandma won't know!"

Anansi took off his hat and filled it full of steaming beans.

As he put the lid back on the beans, he heard shouts from the garden.

"Hey, hey! Get out of Grandma Spider's garden!"

Anansi saw a flock of birds eating the beans
80 he had just planted. Some neighbors were waving and yelling. The scared birds flew through the open kitchen window!

The neighbors ran to the porch and pounded on the door, "Get out of Grandma's kitchen, you nasty birds! Anansi, let us in to help you!"

Anansi didn't know what to do! He had to hide the beans. "Anansi, let us in!" the neighbors yelled. The birds screeched and
90 flapped, and Anansi looked around quickly.

Anansi did the only thing he could think to do. He pulled the hat full of hot beans on his head and opened the door.

Discuss and Decide

Why doesn't Anansi open the door for his neighbors right away? Cite text evidence in your discussion.

The neighbors came in, yelling and screaming and chasing out the flapping birds.

When everything was quiet, they turned to see if Anansi was all right.

There stood Anansi with tears streaming
100 down his face.

"Anansi! Did the birds hurt you, Anansi?"

The birds hadn't touched him, but the hot bean juices soaked his beautiful hair. He tried to sound cheerful when he said, "Thanks, everybody! I'm fine. The birds are gone. You can all go home now."

The neighbors looked at Anansi. "Anansi, what's wrong? Why are you sweating? Were you scared? Were you hurt?"

110 "No, I . . . I'm just hot and sweaty from working in the garden. I have to finish now, so you can go!" The beans were burning Anansi's head and he couldn't stand still. He danced from side to side and up and down, shaking the hat on his head.

"Anansi, that's a wonderful new dance! Let us watch!"

The beans were really burning Anansi's head now. The bean juice was running down
120 his face. He shook his hat and danced until finally he could stand it no more.

"Yeoooow!" Anansi shouted as he pulled the hat from his head. Beans flew everywhere.

Then everyone stared at Anansi in surprise—his head was as bald as an egg! The beans had cooked his hair clean off!

The neighbors began to laugh.

"Look at Anansi! He was hiding beans in his hat and he cooked his hair right off his head!"

130   Anansi was so embarrassed that he ran into the garden and hid in the tall grass until it was dark. He stays in the tall grass a lot these days—and he isn't so crazy about beans anymore.

Discuss and Decide

What happens to Anansi because he was afraid of getting caught eating the beans?

Analyze a Student Model

Read Molly's response to literature closely. The red side notes are the comments that her teacher, Mr. Cummings, wrote.

Molly Ryan

December 12

Blame It on the Beans

Strong details support your statement that Anansi is a good grandson.

When the story starts, Anansi seems like a good grandson. He asks how he can help Grandma Spider. He thanks her when she gives him lemonade. He is respectful and polite. But Anansi's character changes as the story goes on.

Grandma Spider tells Anansi to stay away from the pot of beans. Even though Anansi loves Grandma Spider's spicy beans, he says he understands and he won't go near the pot. He is still respectful and polite.

"However" and "then" are good transition words. Nice work!

Anansi becomes greedy when he smells the beans, however. He knows that he should stay away from them. But he can't! Then smelling the beans is not enough. He eats them.

Anansi knows that eating the beans is bad. But he doesn't feel bad about eating them. He is more worried about getting caught by Grandma Spider. Anansi does not want the neighbors to know he took the beans. He puts the beans on his head to hide them. He lets the beans burn him instead!

Good point. What else shows that his actions are a result of worry about getting caught?

Anansi knew eating the beans was wrong, but he was greedy. He lied to the neighbors about why he was sweating. Anansi should have left the beans alone like Grandma Spider wanted.

Anansi seems like a nice spider at the beginning of this story. But he can't resist tasting his grandma's beans! Anansi loses his hair after he lies about tasting them. The lesson of this story is to be honest and respectful.

That's an important lesson to learn!

Discuss and Decide

Molly writes that the lesson of the story is "to be honest and respectful." Which details in her response to literature support this statement?

Responding to Literature

Literary elements such as characters, settings, and events work together to make a story. After you read, you may be asked to explain how these elements shape a story and how they interact.

Are the story's **characters** believable? Do they talk and act in their own individual ways?

Can a reader picture the story's **setting**? Do the place and time add to the mood and impact events?

Are the story's **events** convincing results of interactions among the characters and the setting?

Essay Tips

Writing a Response to Literature

- Capture your ideas in a strong opening statement.

- Quote from the text to support your ideas.

- Explain how story elements work together.

Look back through *Anansi and the Pot of Beans*. Find one example of how a character's action affects the events of the story. Write the example below.

How does a trickster get what he wants?

You will read:

- **A Greek Fable**
  "The Fox and the Crow"

You will write:

- **A Response to Literature**
  How does a trickster get what he wants?

AS YOU READ You will write a response to the fable below. As you read, underline and circle information that may be useful to you when you write your essay.

The Fox and the Crow

by Aesop

One bright morning as the Fox was following his sharp nose through the wood in search of a bite to eat, he saw a Crow on the limb of a tree overhead. This was by no means the first Crow the Fox had ever seen. What caught his attention this time and made him stop for a second look, was that the lucky Crow held a bit of cheese in her beak.

"No need to search any farther," thought
10 sly Master Fox. "Here is a dainty bite for my breakfast."

Up he trotted to the foot of the tree in which the Crow was sitting, and looking up admiringly, he cried, "Good-morning, beautiful creature!"

The Crow, her head cocked on one side, watched the Fox suspiciously. But she kept her beak tightly closed on the cheese and did not return his greeting.

20 "What a charming creature she is!" said the Fox. "How her feathers shine! What a beautiful form and what splendid wings! Such a wonderful Bird should have a very lovely voice, since everything else about her is so perfect. Could she sing just one song, I know I should hail her Queen of Birds."

Listening to these flattering words, the Crow forgot all her suspicion, and also her breakfast. She wanted very much to be called Queen of
30 Birds.

So she opened her beak wide to utter her loudest caw, and down fell the cheese straight into the Fox's open mouth.

"Thank you," said Master Fox sweetly, as he walked off. "Though it is cracked, you have a voice sure enough, but where are your wits?"

The flatterer lives at the expense of those who will listen to him.

Discuss and Decide

Who is the trickster in this story? How do you know? Cite evidence from the fable in your answer.

Respond to Questions

In Step 2, you have read a fable. Use your notes and refer to the source as you answer the questions. Your answers will help you write your essay.

1 Why does the Fox trick the Crow?

    a. The Fox wants to get even with the Crow.

    b. The Fox has always disliked the Crow.

    c. The Fox doesn't like cheese.

    d. The Fox wants the Crow's cheese.

2 How does the Fox get the cheese from the Crow?

    a. He greets the Crow when he sees her.

    b. He asks the Crow to sing.

    c. He makes a trade for the cheese.

    d. He knocks the cheese out of the tree.

3 What does the word *suspicion* mean in line 28?

    a. distrust

    b. anger

    c. confusion

    d. hunger

4 **Prose Constructed-Response** How does the Crow's opinion of the Fox change during the story? Cite text evidence in your response.

_____

_____

_____

_____

5 **Prose Constructed-Response** Think about the setting of the fable. Why is it important that the Crow is in a tree for the Fox's plan to work?

_____

_____

_____

_____

6 **Prose Constructed-Response** What lesson does the fable teach? Cite text evidence in your answer.

_____

_____

_____

_____

Planning and Prewriting

Before you draft your essay, complete some important planning steps.

Before you start writing, determine your main idea. Look for supporting details to include in your essay. Complete the chart below to help you think about the events in the story.

Assignment
Write a response to literature to answer the question: How does a trickster get what he wants?

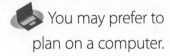 You may prefer to plan on a computer.

Examine Key Events

Event	What the Fox Plans	How the Crow Responds
The Fox greets the Crow.		
The Fox asks the Crow to sing.		

Finalize Your Plan

You know what you want to say in your response to the fable. Now, it's time to plan the structure of your essay. You will save time and create a more organized, logical essay by planning the structure before you start writing.

Use your responses and notes from pp. 100–102 to complete the graphic organizer.

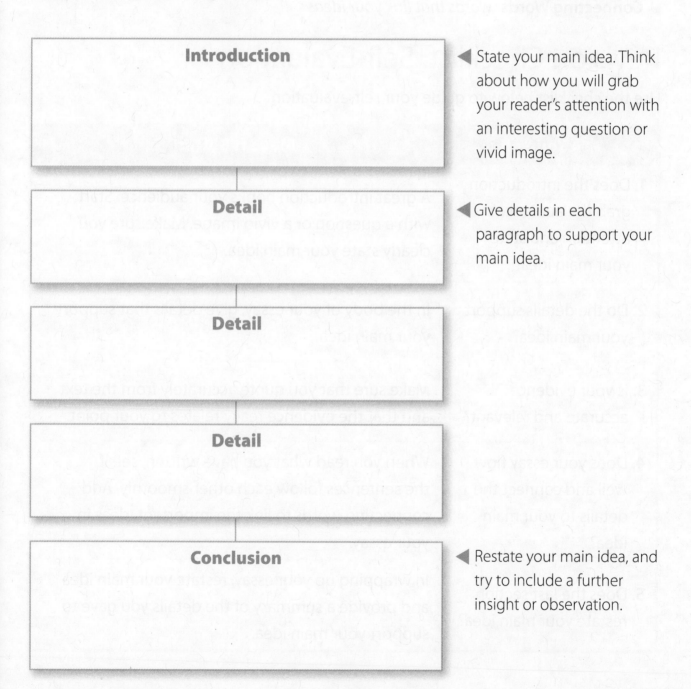

Introduction

◀ State your main idea. Think about how you will grab your reader's attention with an interesting question or vivid image.

Detail

◀ Give details in each paragraph to support your main idea.

Detail

Detail

Conclusion

◀ Restate your main idea, and try to include a further insight or observation.

Draft Your Essay

If you drafted your essay on the computer, you may wish to print it out.

As you write, think about:

▶ **Purpose** *to express your ideas about a work of literature*

▶ **Clarity** *ideas that are straightforward and understandable*

▶ **Support** *examples from the sources that support your ideas*

▶ **Organization** *the logical structure for your essay*

▶ **Connecting Words** *words that link your ideas*

Revision Checklist: Self-Evaluation

Use the checklist below to guide your self-evaluation.

Ask Yourself	Make It Better
1. Does the introduction grab the audience's attention and state your main idea?	A great introduction hooks your audience. Start with a question or a vivid image. Make sure you clearly state your main idea.
2. Do the details support your main idea?	In the body of your essay, give details that support your main idea.
3. Is your evidence accurate and relevant?	Make sure that you quote accurately from the text and that the evidence really relates to your point.
4. Does your essay flow well and connect the details to your main idea?	When you read what you have written, see if the sentences follow each other smoothly. Add connecting words to link the important ideas in your essay.
5. Does the last section restate your main idea?	In wrapping up your essay, restate your main idea and provide a summary of the details you gave to support your main idea.

Revision Checklist: Peer Review

Exchange your essay with a classmate, or read it out loud to your partner. As you read and comment on your partner's essay, focus on organization and evidence. Help your partner find parts of the draft that need to be revised.

What to Look For	Notes for My Partner
1. Does the introduction grab the audience's attention and state the main idea?	
2. Do the details support the main idea?	
3. Is the evidence accurate and relevant?	
4. Does the essay flow well and connect the details to the main idea?	
5. Does the last section restate the main idea?	

Support Your Ideas!

Review Your Use of Text Evidence

When you write a response to literature, the best way to support your ideas is to cite evidence from the literature itself. You can use quotes, give examples from the text, or tell what the characters say, think, or feel.

This paragraph was written about "The Fox and the Crow." There is no direct evidence from the source material, but there is a lot of the writer's opinion.

> The Fox wants the cheese. He thinks he is smarter than the Crow, and he proves it by making her sing. He always was a great trickster.

The paragraph can be improved by using quotes from the source to support the writer's idea.

> The Fox uses flattery and wits to get the cheese from the Crow. The Crow believes the flattery. The Fox calls her "beautiful," and she wants "to be called Queen of Birds," so the Crow sings and drops the cheese.

Cite from the Source

- State your ideas clearly, with no room for confusion.
- Support your ideas with evidence from the source material.
- Don't use unsupported opinions or assume that your audience already knows all the information that you know.

Edit

Edit your essay to correct spelling, grammar, and punctuation errors.

What are the character traits of a trickster?

You will read:

- **An American Indian Trickster Tale**

  Turtle Races with Beaver

You will write:

- **A Response to Literature**

  What are the character traits of a trickster?

AS YOU READ

Pay attention to the characters' thoughts, words, and actions. Make notes about information you find useful.

Notes

Turtle Races with Beaver

retold by Michael J. Caduto and Joseph Bruchac

Long ago, Turtle lived in a small pond. It was a fine place. There were alder trees along the bank to give shade and a fine grassy bank where Turtle could crawl out and sun himself. There were plenty of fish for Turtle to catch. The small pond had everything any turtle could ever want, and Turtle thought his pond was the finest place in the whole world. Turtle spent his time swimming around, sunning

10 himself, and catching fish whenever he was hungry. So it went until the cold winds began to blow down from the north.

"Ah," Turtle said, "It is time for me to go to sleep." Then he dove down to the bottom of the pond and burrowed into the mud. He went to sleep for the winter. He slept so soundly, in fact,

that he slept a little later than usual and did not wake up until it was late in the spring. The warming waters of the pond woke him, and
20 he crawled out of the mud and began to swim toward the surface. Something was wrong, though, for it seemed to take much too long to get to the surface of his small pond. Turtle was certain the water had not been that deep when he went to sleep.

Close Read

What does Turtle like about his pond?

As soon as Turtle reached the surface and looked around, he saw that things were not as they should be. His small pond was more than twice its normal

30 size. His fine grassy bank for sunning himself was underwater! His beautiful alder trees had been cut down and made into a big dam.

"Who has done this to my pond?" Turtle said.

Just then Turtle heard a loud sound. WHAP! Turtle turned to look and saw

40 a strange animal swimming toward him across the surface of his pond. It had a big, flat tail and as it came close to Turtle, it lifted up that big, flat tail and hit the surface of the water with it. WHAP!

"Who are you?" Turtle said. "What are you doing in my pond? What have you done to my beautiful trees?"

"Hunh!" the strange animal said. "This is not your pond. This is my pond! I am Beaver

50 and I cut down those trees with my teeth and I built that dam and made this pond nice and deep. This is my pond and you must leave."

"No," Turtle said. "This is my pond. If you do not leave, I will fight you. I am a great warrior."

"Hunh!" Beaver said. "That is good. Let us fight. I will call all my relatives to help me, and they will chew your head off with their strong teeth."

60   Turtle looked closely at Beaver's teeth. They were long and yellow and looked very sharp.

"Hah!" Turtle said. "I can see it would be too easy to fight you. Instead we should have a contest to decide which of us will leave this pond forever."

"Hunh!" Beaver said. "That is a good idea. Let us see who can stay underwater the longest. I can stay under for a whole day."

Close Read

Why does Beaver want to stay in the pond?

_____

_____

As soon as Beaver said that, Turtle saw he
70 would have to think of a different contest.
He had been about to suggest that they see
who could stay underwater the longest, but if
what Beaver said was true, then he would beat
Turtle.

"Hah!" Turtle said. "It would be too easy to
defeat you that way. Let us have a race instead.
The first one to reach the other side of the
pond is the winner. The loser must leave my
pond forever."

80 "Hunh!" Beaver said. "That is a good
contest. I am the fastest swimmer of all. When
I win, you will have to leave my pond forever.
Let us begin to race."

"Wait," Turtle said, "I am such a fast
swimmer that it would not be fair unless I
started from behind you."

Then Turtle placed himself behind Beaver,
right next to Beaver's big tail.

"I am ready," Turtle said, "let us begin!"

90 Beaver began to swim. He was such a fast swimmer that Turtle could barely keep up with him. When they were halfway across the pond, Turtle began to fall even further behind. But Turtle had a plan. He stuck his long neck out and grabbed Beaver's tail in his jaws.

Beaver felt something grab his tail, but he could not look back. He was too busy swimming, trying to win the race. He swung his tail back and forth, but Turtle held on tight.

100 Now Beaver was almost to the other side of the pond. Turtle bit down even harder. Beaver swung his tail high up into the air, trying to shake free whatever had hold of him. Just as Beaver's tail reached the top of its swing, Turtle let go. He flew through the air and landed on the bank! Beaver looked up, and there was Turtle! Turtle had won the race.

Discuss and Decide

Why does Beaver agree to race Turtle?

So it was that Beaver had to leave and Turtle, once again, had his pond to himself. With its
110 new deeper waters there were soon even more fish than there had been before and Turtle's alders grew back once more. Truly, Turtle's pond was the finest place in the whole world.

Discuss and Decide

How is Turtle's situation at the end of the story similar to his situation at the beginning?

Respond to Questions

These questions will help you think about the source you've read. Use your notes and refer to the source to answer the questions. Your answers to these questions will help you write your essay.

1 Which word best describes Turtle?

   a. sad

   b. careless

   c. scared

   d. clever

2 Which sentence best supports your answer to Question 1?

   a. "Turtle spent his time swimming . . ." (lines 8–9)

   b. "I am a great warrior." (lines 54–55)

   c. ". . . Turtle could barely keep up . . ." (line 91)

   d. ". . . Turtle had a plan." (line 94)

3 Why doesn't Turtle want to fight Beaver?

   a. Beaver's teeth are long and sharp.

   b. Turtle doesn't want the pond anymore.

   c. Turtle knows he will win if he fights Beaver.

   d. Beaver says he will give the pond to Turtle.

4 Why does Turtle challenge Beaver to a race?

   a. He knows he is faster than Beaver.

   b. He wants to be friends with Beaver.

   c. He has a plan to win.

   d. He doesn't want to leave the pond.

5 Prose Constructed-Response Why does Turtle want to live in the pond? Cite text evidence in your response.

_____

_____

_____

_____

6 Prose Constructed-Response How does Turtle trick Beaver? Cite text evidence in your response.

_____

_____

_____

_____

7 Prose Constructed-Response How do events in the story affect the setting? Cite text evidence in your response.

_____

_____

_____

_____

1. Analyze   2. Practice   **3. Perform**

Write the Essay

Read the assignment.

Assignment
Write a response to literature that answers the question: What are the character traits of a trickster?

Plan

Use the graphic organizer to help you outline the structure of your response to literature.

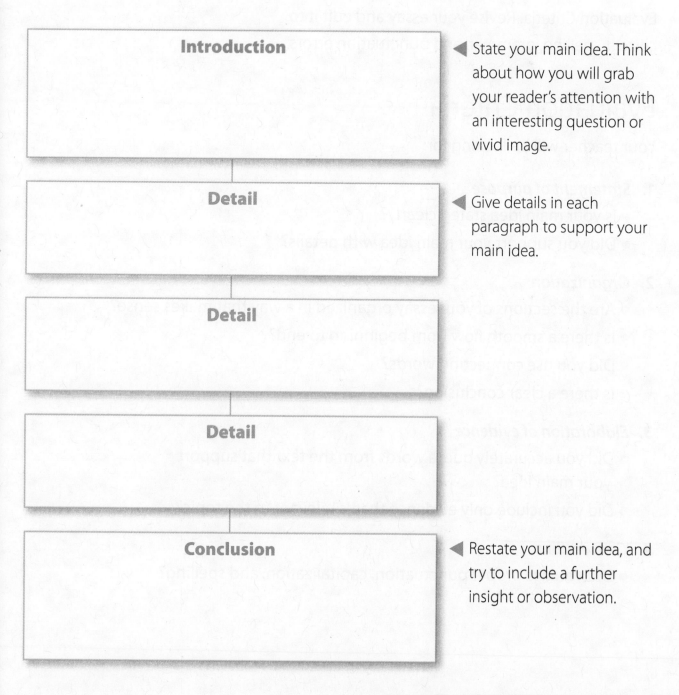

Introduction

◀ State your main idea. Think about how you will grab your reader's attention with an interesting question or vivid image.

Detail

◀ Give details in each paragraph to support your main idea.

Detail

Detail

Conclusion

◀ Restate your main idea, and try to include a further insight or observation.

Draft

Use your notes and completed graphic organizer to write a first draft of your response to literature.

Revise and Edit

Look back over your essay and compare it to the Evaluation Criteria. Revise your essay and edit it to correct spelling, grammar, and punctuation errors.

You may wish to draft and edit your essay on the computer.

Evaluation Criteria

Your teacher will be looking for:

1. *Statement of purpose*
   - Is your main idea stated clearly?
   - Did you support your main idea with details?

2. *Organization*
   - Are the sections of your essay organized in a way that makes sense?
   - Is there a smooth flow from beginning to end?
   - Did you use connecting words?
   - Is there a clear conclusion?

3. *Elaboration of evidence*
   - Did you accurately quote words from the text that support your main idea?
   - Did you include only evidence that is relevant to the topic?

4. *Conventions*
   - Did you use proper punctuation, capitalization, and spelling?

Strange Situations

Unit 4
Narrative

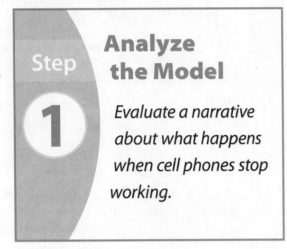

Step 1

Analyze the Model

Evaluate a narrative about what happens when cell phones stop working.

Step 2

Practice the Task

Write a narrative about what happens when an ostrich visits your home.

Step 3

Perform the Task

Write a narrative about what happens when you develop an animal's ability.

A narrative tells about a series of events. Some narratives discuss real events while others are made-up stories. But stories from a writer's imagination can still be believable.

An actual person, a true event, or interesting information can inspire someone to write. Many writers will base a made-up story on something that actually happened. For example, a writer might see a news report about a heroic dog and wonder what other deeds that dog might do. The writer might read more sources on heroic dogs and then write a story based on those sources.

When you read sources on a topic before you write, your story will be more convincing. Your readers will appreciate that the events in your story seem real.

IN THIS UNIT, you will evaluate a story about what happens when a tool that everyone relies on no longer works. Then you will read two informational sources and write a story about what happens when you have a large animal guest at home. Finally, you will read two sources and write a story about what happens when you are given a special power.

What happens when cell phones don't work?

You will read:

- **Two Fact Sheets**

  How Do Cell Phones Work?

  What Does Your Cell Phone Do?

You will analyze:

- **A Student Model**

  The Day Cell Phones Stopped Working

Source 1: Fact Sheet

Mr. Pham's student, Adrien De Vos, used this fact sheet as one of the sources for his narrative about what happens when cell phones don't work. As you read, make notes in the side columns. Underline information that you find useful.

Notes

How Do Cell Phones Work?

When you talk into a cell phone, a microphone inside the phone changes your voice into electrical signals, which are sent out as radio waves. The waves travel to a cellular tower. It passes them on to the person you are calling. When the signal reaches the person, it is turned back into sound. You can now have a conversation! Cell phones can't be used on some airplanes and in some hospitals, in case they interfere with the electronics being used. And cell phones often don't work underground.

Payphones

Payphones are public telephones that require money to make a phone call. As cell phones become more popular, payphones aren't used as much. There used to be more than 2 million payphones in the U.S. Now there are fewer than 250,000.

Landlines

A landline is a telephone that is connected to another location by a cable laid across land. In the past, many homes in the U.S. had landlines. Today, many people rely on cell phones as their only phones. Most businesses still rely on landlines.

Source 2: Fact Sheet

Adrien used this fact sheet as a second source for his narrative. Continue to make notes in the side columns as you read. Underline information that you find helpful.

Notes

What Does Your Cell Phone Do?

Cell phones allow you to make phone calls. But with certain models of phones, known as smart phones, you may be able to do many of the following things:

Send text messages	Check email
Listen to music	Take notes
Use GPS (Global Positioning System) **and maps**	Check the weather
Read newspapers, magazines, or books	Take photos
Set an alarm	Shoot and edit videos
Play games	Go on the Internet

Notes

Close Read

What are the main differences between cell phones and landlines?

Analyze a Student Model

After the class read the fact sheets, Mr. Pham asked his students to write a narrative about what would happen if cell phones stopped working. Read Adrien's narrative closely. The red side notes are the comments that Mr. Pham wrote.

Adrien De Vos

February 3

The Day Cell Phones Stopped Working

This opening really grabs my attention.

"I can't stream my music! What's going on?" Suresh asked. No one's cell phone was working. Our bus driver stopped the bus and told us to wait while he checked things out.

"I need to call my mom to let her know I'm okay!" My friend Billy said. "We have a landline at home. I'll call her from a payphone. Maybe we can find one!" Then he ran out of the bus. I ran after him.

"Then" is a good word to show the order of events.

People were talking in groups. Some were shouting.

1. Analyze   2. Practice   3. Perform

"Help!" One woman cried. "Concert tickets are going on sale in five minutes, and I can't access the Internet!"

"What's going on with the phones?" I asked. No one answered. A man yelled about losing his turn in the game he was playing. Another woman threw her phone on the ground. Billy and I kept looking for a payphone. We ran through knots of people who were just standing still. They were staring at their phone screens in confusion. We ran for ten minutes. We didn't see any payphones.

"Wait!" I said. "We can go into a store. Stores have landlines! I'm glad we know where we are. We don't need the GPS on our cell phones."

We ran into our local grocery store. Mr. Andrews asked us why we had been running.

"Didn't you hear? Cell phones aren't working!" Billy said.

"Oh, I don't own a cell phone. That doesn't bother me," Mr. Andrews said. He let Billy use the landline. Billy dialed, listened, turned back to me, and told me that he had to leave a message on the answering machine.

"What's an answering machine?'" I asked.

Discuss and Decide

How did Adrien include information from the sources to make his narrative believable?

Set the Scene!

The setting is the time and place of the action in a story. A good writer will include memorable images and concrete details to make the setting come alive. In his story, Adrien could have described the setting more realistically so that the reader could picture where the action takes place.

Here is a part of Adrien's story:

> We ran for ten minutes. We didn't see any payphones.

How could Adrien describe the scene better? He could supply details that let the reader "see" the setting. Here's an example:

> We ran from block to block for ten minutes. Every corner that would have been a perfect spot for a payphone was just a patch of bare concrete.

Story Tips — Remember These Tips!

- Imagine the setting in your mind. Then, try to put it down in words. Do your words accurately describe what you are thinking of?

- Imagine that a reader will draw a picture based on your words. Would it look like the setting you are writing about?

Look back through Adrien's story. Find one description of the setting that you could improve. Rewrite the description and exchange your work with a partner. Ask your partner if your writing lets him or her better imagine the setting.

What happens when an ostrich visits your house?

You will read:

- **A Fact Sheet**
  All About Ostriches

- **A Floor Plan**
  Around the House

You will write:

- **A Narrative**
  What happens when an ostrich visits your house?

Source 1: Fact Sheet

AS YOU READ You will write a narrative about what would happen if an ostrich visited your home. As you read, underline information that may be useful to you when you write your story.

All About Ostriches

- While many birds can fly, ostriches cannot.

- Ostriches are the world's largest birds. An ostrich can grow to be 9 feet tall.

- Ostriches are the heaviest birds. An ostrich can weigh up to 350 pounds.

- Ostriches are fast! An ostrich can run up to 43 miles an hour.

- Ostriches are omnivores. This means that they eat plants and animals.

- Ostriches have a claw on each foot. They can defend themselves from predators, such as lions, with these sharp claws and with kicks from their powerful legs.

1. Analyze   **2. Practice**   3. Perform

- Wild ostriches can be found on the African savanna and in desert lands.

- Ostriches usually live in herds of less than 10 birds.

- Ostriches have the biggest eyes of any land animal.

That's a Myth!

You may have heard that ostriches bury their heads in the sand. It may look like an ostrich has his head buried when he hides from a predator. This is because he lies down low, and presses his neck into the ground to better hide himself.

Source 2: Floor Plan

The floor plan below shows the layout of a modern apartment and some items you might find in the rooms. Use the plan to help you come up with ideas about what might happen if an ostrich visited where you live.

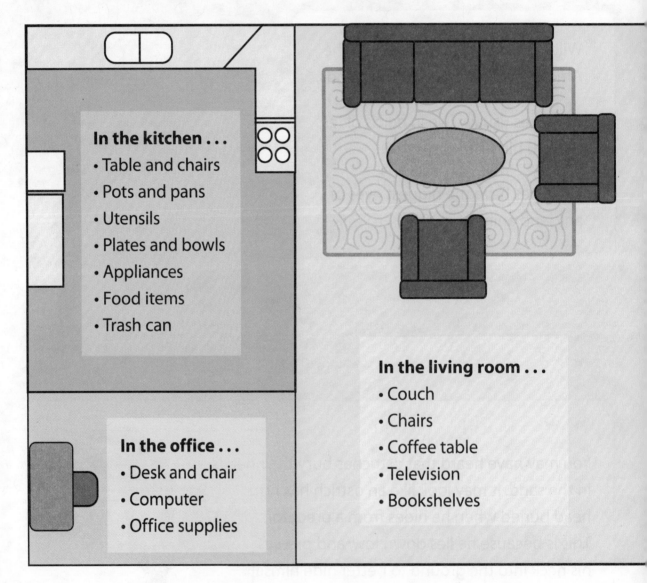

Around the House

In the kitchen . . .
- Table and chairs
- Pots and pans
- Utensils
- Plates and bowls
- Appliances
- Food items
- Trash can

In the office . . .
- Desk and chair
- Computer
- Office supplies

In the living room . . .
- Couch
- Chairs
- Coffee table
- Television
- Bookshelves

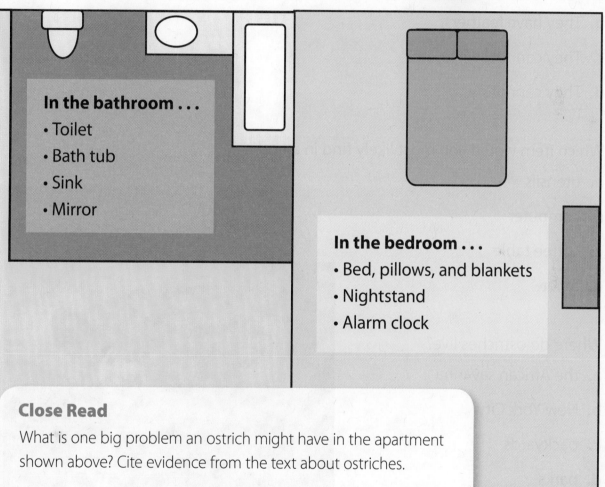

In the bathroom . . .
- Toilet
- Bath tub
- Sink
- Mirror

In the bedroom . . .
- Bed, pillows, and blankets
- Nightstand
- Alarm clock

Close Read

What is one big problem an ostrich might have in the apartment shown above? Cite evidence from the text about ostriches.

Respond to Questions

In Step 2, you have read a fact sheet and looked at a
floor plan. Use your notes and refer to the sources as you
answer the questions. Your answers will help you write
your narrative.

① According to Source 1, what is one way that ostriches
are different from other birds?

   a. They have teeth.

   b. They have feathers.

   c. They cannot swim.

   d. They cannot fly.

② Which item would you most likely find in an office?

   a. utensils

   b. computer

   c. coffee table

   d. toilet

③ Where do ostriches live?

   a. the African savanna

   b. New York City

   c. backyards

   d. parks

4 **Prose Constructed-Response** What dangers might an ostrich face in an apartment that it would not face where it usually lives?

_____

_____

_____

_____

5 **Prose Constructed-Response** Which room in the floor plan might an ostrich like the best? Explain, using evidence from the sources.

_____

_____

_____

_____

6 **Prose Constructed-Response** Explain how the pictures of ostriches add to your understanding of why an ostrich might cause problems in a house.

_____

_____

_____

_____

Planning and Prewriting

Before you draft your narrative, complete some important planning steps.

Assignment
Write a narrative about what happens when an ostrich visits your house.

You may prefer to plan on a computer.

Collect Information

Before you start writing, think about the sources you've read. Look for interesting facts and details that you can include in your narrative. Complete the chart below with information from each source.

Source	Interesting Facts to Use in My Narrative
Fact Sheet All About Ostriches	
Floor Plan Around the House	

Finalize Your Plan

You know what you want to include in your narrative. Now, it's time to plan the structure of your story. You will save time and create a more organized, logical narrative by planning the structure before you start writing.

Use your responses and notes from pp. 134–136 to complete the graphic organizer.

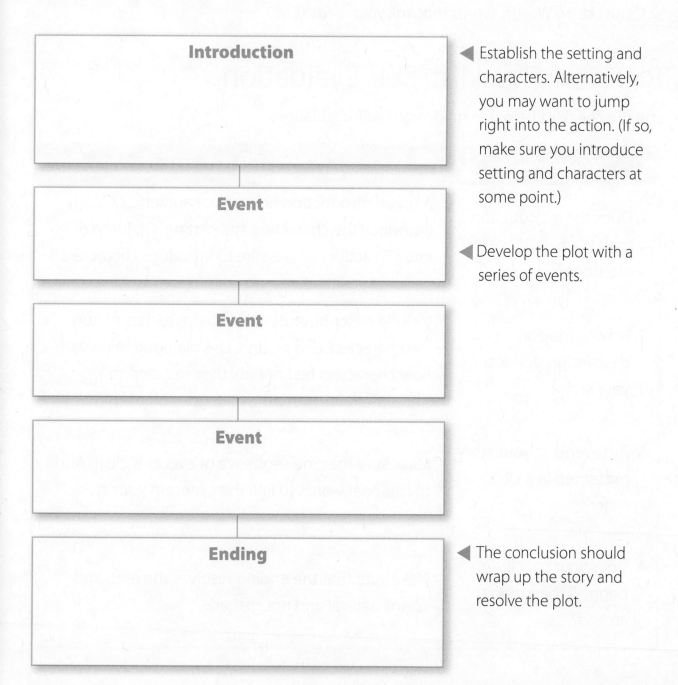

Introduction — ◀ Establish the setting and characters. Alternatively, you may want to jump right into the action. (If so, make sure you introduce setting and characters at some point.)

Event

Event — ◀ Develop the plot with a series of events.

Event

Ending — ◀ The conclusion should wrap up the story and resolve the plot.

Draft Your Narrative

If you drafted your story on the computer, you may wish to print it out.

As you write, think about:

▶ **Purpose** *to entertain or engage the reader*

▶ **Clarity** *straightforward, understandable ideas and descriptions*

▶ **Support** *factual details that help make your story believable*

▶ **Organization** *the logical structure for your story*

▶ **Connecting Words** *words that link your ideas*

Revision Checklist: Self-Evaluation

Use the checklist below to guide your self-evaluation.

Ask Yourself	Make It Better
1. Does the introduction grab your audience's attention?	A great introduction hooks your audience. Clearly introduce the characters and setting. Or, jump right into the action. (Make sure to introduce characters and setting later.)
2. Do dialogue and description develop your story?	Include descriptive details to help readers picture the characters and setting. Use dialogue to reveal how characters feel or how they respond to situations. Make sure the dialogue sounds natural.
3. Are events in your story presented in a clear order?	Make sure that the sequence of events is clear. Add transitional words to link the events in your story.
4. Does your conclusion bring all the action to an end?	Make sure that the ending resolves the plot, and seems natural and not rushed.

Revision Checklist: Peer Review

Exchange your story with a classmate, or read it out loud to your partner. As you read and comment on your partner's story, focus on the elements of a good narrative. Help your partner find parts of the draft that need to be revised.

What to Look For	Notes for My Partner
1. Does the introduction grab the audience's attention?	
2. Do dialogue and description develop the story?	
3. Are events in the story presented in a clear order?	
4. Does the conclusion bring all the action to an end?	

Writing Dialogue

Dialogue is conversation between two or more characters in a story. It can be used to reveal the characters' personalities, explain situations, and move events along. It can also be used to reveal important details about those situations and events.

This example of dialogue explains a situation:

"Jake, is that you?" a voice called from the kitchen.

"Mom?" I asked as I walked into the room. "What are you doing up so late?"

"I heard a noise, and I saw a trail of feathers leading to the refrigerator," she said. "Did you and Sara have a pillow fight?"

Story Tips

Remember These Tips When Writing Dialogue

- Words that characters say appear in quotation marks. Make sure that it's clear who is speaking.

- One character may not know everything that another character knows. Be sure your dialogue reflects the characters' knowledge of events in the story.

- Make sure the dialogue adds something to the story. It might reveal how characters feel or explain the action.

Edit

Edit your essay to correct spelling, grammar, and punctuation errors.

1. Analyze   **2. Practice**   3. Perform

What happens when you develop an animal's abilities?

You will read:

- **An Informative Essay**

  Imagine That!

- **An Infographic**

  Found in the Wild

You will write:

- **A Narrative**

  What happens when you develop an animal's abilities?

Source 1: Informative Essay

AS YOU READ
Think about which facts you could use in your narrative as you read the sources. Make notes about information you find useful.

Notes

Imagine That!

Humans can see, smell, taste, hear, and touch. But did you know that animals have these same senses, and that some of theirs work even better than ours? Some of these animals you may even have in your home! Dogs, for example, can smell more than 10,000 times better than humans. Imagine being able to identify things
10   by smell alone!

Have you ever wanted to be invisible? Chameleons can change their colors to blend in with their surroundings. Chameleons will change colors to hide from predators or to communicate with other chameleons.

You or someone you know may have a cat. A house cat is fast, but not as fast as a cheetah.
20   A cheetah can run faster than 60 miles an hour. It can reach that speed—from resting—in only

three seconds! That's super speed. All cats,
both housecats and wild cats, can see in almost
complete darkness. They have built-in night vision!

You may have seen different types of birds
flying in your neighborhood. Most of these birds
fly around from tree to tree. Seeing the peregrine
falcon is something else entirely. The peregrine is
the fastest animal in the world. When a peregrine
30 is diving from the sky while hunting prey on the
ground, it can go as fast as 200 miles an hour!
Peregrine falcons that migrate from one place to
another can fly as many as 15,500 miles in a year.
That's a lot of flying!
Peregrine falcons can
see details three times
finer than humans
can. Imagine how
much the peregrine
40 falcon sees while it is
high in the sky!

Found in the Wild

Bat

- The bat is the only mammal that can fly.

- Bats use a sense called echolocation to help them "see." The bat sends out a series of short bursts of sound as it flies. When the sound waves hit an object, such as prey, they will bounce back to the bat. The bat can tell where the object is and how big it is.

Sperm Whale

- The sperm whale has the largest brain of any animal on Earth.

- The sperm whale can hold its breath for up to 90 minutes. (The record for a human is 22 minutes.)

Armadillo

- The armadillo is the only living mammal that is covered in a shell of bony plates. These bony plates cover its head, back, legs, and tail.

- The three-banded armadillo can curl itself into a ball to cover itself completely in its bony plates. Its "armor" can then protect it from predators.

African Elephant

- The largest land animal on Earth is the African elephant. It can be up to 13 feet tall and weigh up to 14,000 pounds.

- The African elephant can lift over 550 pounds.

Close Read

Pick one animal from Source 1 or Source 2. Why might someone want to have that animal's ability?

_____

_____

Respond to Questions

These questions will help you think about the sources you've read. Use your notes and refer to the sources to answer the questions. Your answers will help you write your narrative.

1 Which of these animals is the fastest?

   a. armadillo

   b. chameleon

   c. peregrine falcon

   d. dog

2 Which animals' abilities would help you at night?

   a. bats and cats

   b. bats and falcons

   c. cats and dogs

   d. armadillos and elephants

3 Which sentence from Source 1 explains an ability of a chameleon?

   a. "... change colors to hide from predators ..."

   b. "That's super speed."

   c. "They have built-in night vision!"

   d. "... can see details three times finer than humans can."

4 Which animal's ability would be most helpful if you needed to lift something heavy?

   a. cheetah

   b. cat

   c. peregrine falcon

   d. African elephant

5 **Prose Constructed-Response** How is a sperm whale's ability to hold its breath underwater different from a human's? Cite evidence from the text in your response.

_____

_____

_____

_____

_____

_____

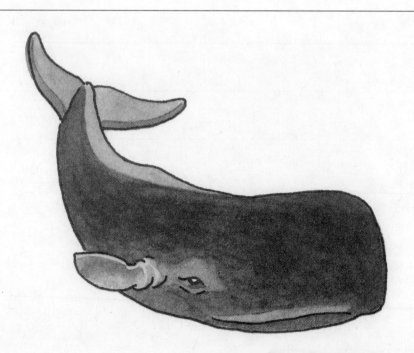

6 **Prose Constructed-Response** Which source would you cite for information on the largest land animal in the world? Cite text evidence in your response.

_____

_____

_____

_____

7 **Prose Constructed-Response** Explain which animals' abilities give them an advantage at night. Cite evidence from the text in your response.

_____

_____

_____

_____

Write the Narrative

Read the assignment.

Assignment
Write a narrative about what happens when you suddenly develop an animal's abilities.

Plan

Use the graphic organizer to help you outline the structure of your narrative.

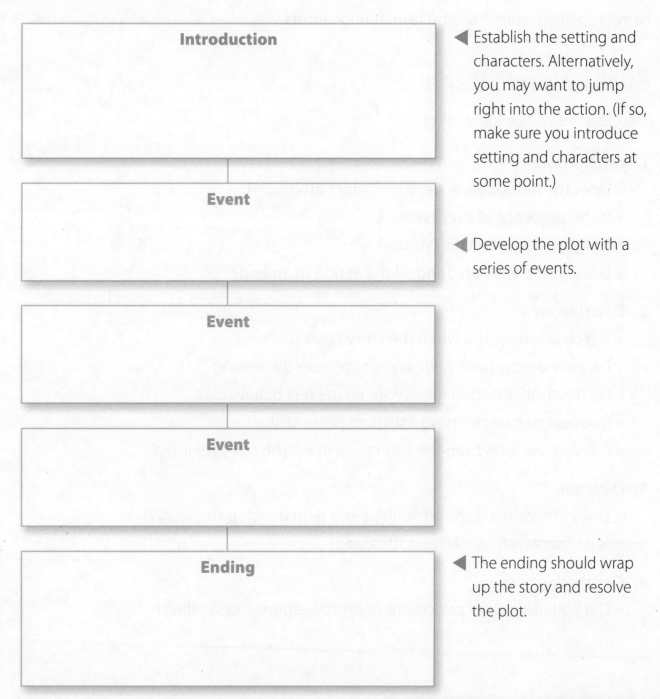

Introduction ◀ Establish the setting and characters. Alternatively, you may want to jump right into the action. (If so, make sure you introduce setting and characters at some point.)

Event

Event ◀ Develop the plot with a series of events.

Event

Ending ◀ The ending should wrap up the story and resolve the plot.

Draft

Use your notes and completed graphic organizer
to write a first draft of your narrative.

Revise and Edit

Look back over your story and compare it to the
Evaluation Criteria. Revise your story and edit it to
correct spelling, grammar, and punctuation errors.

You may wish to
draft and edit your story
on the computer.

Evaluation Criteria

Your teacher will be looking for:

1. **Organization**
   - Does the introduction get the reader's attention?
   - Is the sequence of events clear?
   - Did you use connecting words?
   - Does the conclusion bring all the action to an end?

2. **Descriptions**
   - Is it clear where and when the story takes place?
   - Do your descriptions help a reader picture the setting?
   - Do descriptive details make your characters believable?
   - Does each character have a distinct personality?
   - Did you use facts from the sources to make the story realistic?

3. **Dialogue**
   - Does the dialogue sound realistic and help develop the story?
   - Is it clear which character is speaking?

4. **Conventions**
   - Did you use proper punctuation, capitalization, and spelling?

On Your Own

Mixed Practice

Task 1

Research Simulation
Opinion Essay
Should children do chores?

Task 2

Research Simulation
Informative Essay
How and why do the members of an animal group cooperate with each other?

Task 3

Response to Literature
How do Odysseus and his men use a plan to trick the Trojans?

Task 4

Research Simulation
Narrative
What does a child experience on the Oregon trail?

Research Simulation

Opinion Essay

Your Assignment

You will read two texts on chores. Then you will write an opinion essay about whether children should do chores.

Time Management: Opinion Essay Task

There are two parts to most formal writing tests. Both parts of the tests are timed, so it's important to use your limited time wisely.

Part 1: Read Sources

(35)

Preview the Assignment

35 minutes

You will have 35 minutes to read two texts about whether children should do chores. You will then answer questions about the sources.

How Many?

How many pages of reading?

How many multiple-choice questions?

How many prose constructed-response questions?

How do you plan to use the 35 minutes?

Estimated time to read:

  "Children Should Do Chores"   minutes

  "Our Children Don't Need Chores"   minutes

Estimated time to answer questions?   minutes

Total   **35** minutes

35 minutes! That's not much time.

Preview the questions. This will help you know which information you'll need to find as you read.

This is a lot to do in a short time.

Underline and take notes as you read. You probably won't have time to reread.

Part 2: Write the Essay

Plan and Write an Opinion Essay

85 minutes

You will have 85 minutes to plan, write, revise, and edit your essay.

> How much time do you have? Pay attention to the clock!

Your Plan

Before you start to write, decide on your opinion. Then think about the reasons and evidence you will use to support your opinion.

How do you plan to use the 85 minutes?

Estimated time for planning the essay? ☐ minutes

Estimated time for writing? ☐ minutes

> Be sure to leave enough time for this step!

Estimated time for editing? ☐ minutes

Estimated time for checking spelling, grammar, and punctuation? ☐ minutes

Total   **85** minutes

> Reread your essay, making sure that the points are clear. Check that there are no spelling or punctuation mistakes.

Your Assignment

> You will read two texts and then write an
> opinion essay about whether children should
> do chores.

Complete the following steps as you plan and compose
your essay.

1. Read an editorial about why children should do chores.

2. Read an editorial about why children shouldn't do chores.

3. Answer questions about the sources.

4. Plan, write, and revise your essay.

Part 1 (35 minutes)

You will now read the sources. Take notes on important
facts and details as you read. You can refer to the sources
and your notes as you write your essay.

Children Should Do Chores

By Maggie Aldrich

Children should do chores. They teach children why it is important to help others. They encourage children to do something useful for everyone at home. Chores teach children discipline and responsibility. These are important skills for everyone to learn.

Many children live with their families. Adults do most of the chores for the whole family. It is not fair to expect the adults to do
10 all of the work around the house. Children go to school during the day, and adults go to work. Both adults and children are tired when they get home, and they want to play or relax. If everyone helps out with the chores, they will be

done faster and everybody will have more time to do the things they want to do.

Chores don't have to be boring. There are ways to make chores fun. Sing and dance around when you dust or vacuum. Adults and
20 children can also rotate some chores. Switch chores every month or every week. That way, no one will get stuck with a chore he or she doesn't like for a long time.

Chores are helpful practice for the future! When you are an adult, you have to do chores whether you like them or not. There may not be anyone around to ask to do them for you. Learning how to finish chores will help children later in life.

30 Believe it or not, some children actually enjoy doing chores. My nephew helps his mother around the house. He sets the table for meals and he helps to clear the table. He matches up socks when it's laundry day. His mother never has to ask him to do these chores. He just likes to help. He has been doing chores for some time, so they are just another part of the routine.

Chores are good for us. They don't have to
40 be a boring task. We should think of them as a way for us to help one another. When we work together to finish chores, we all have more free time to spend with each other and to do the things we like.

Our Children Don't Need Chores

By Manuel Vilan

Children already have enough responsibility. They don't need to do chores. Why should we ask our children to do things we don't want to do?

Today our children are a lot busier than we were. They don't have the time to do chores. They have homework and after-school activities. My daughter, for example, goes to soccer practice right after school. She plays
10 for two hours every day and then goes home to do homework. By the time she is done with homework it's dark out, and she's too tired to do anything but go to bed.

Children should be able to enjoy their free time. They are only young once. They should be doing fun things, like playing outside, building a fort, or painting a picture. When you are an adult, you might not have time for the fun stuff. Let the children have their fun!

20 Most children don't want to do chores. Making them do chores only causes them to be unhappy with adults for making them do something that is an adult responsibility. It is my job as a parent to take care of my family. My daughter doesn't have to set the table for dinner because I can do that chore. She will learn how to do these things by watching me and other adults.

Children can't even do some of the chores 30 at home. The garbage bag might be bigger than they are! In the time it takes to teach someone else how to do a chore, I can do it. I don't need to spend the time telling someone else what to do.

Children will learn how to do tasks as they grow up. We do not need to force them to do chores while they are still young. There is plenty of time for our children to learn how to do things for themselves and for others.

Am I on Track?

Actual Time Spent Reading

Questions

Answer the following questions. You may refer to your reading notes, and you should cite text evidence in your responses. Your answers to these questions will be scored. You will be able to refer to your answers as you write your essay in Part 2.

1 The word *rotate* is used in the source called "Children Should Do Chores." What choice has the same meaning as *rotate*?

   a. run

   b. change

   c. talk about

   d. throw away

2 **Prose Constructed-Response** According to "Children Should Do Chores," what are two skills that children learn from doing chores?

_____

_____

_____

_____

3 **Prose Constructed-Response** What is one reason why the author of "Our Children Don't Need Chores" thinks chores are an adult responsibility?

_____

_____

_____

Part 2 (85 minutes)

You now have 85 minutes to review your notes and the sources and to plan, draft, revise, and edit your essay. While you may use your notes and refer to the sources, your essay must represent your original work. You may refer to your responses to the questions in Part 1, but you cannot change those answers. Now read your assignment and begin your work.

Your assignment

You have read two sources about chores. Each text discusses whether or not children should do chores. The two texts are:

- "Children Should Do Chores"
- "Our Children Don't Need Chores"

Consider the opinions presented in the texts on whether children should do chores.

Write an essay that gives your opinion on whether children should do chores. Remember to use reasons and evidence to support your opinion.

Now begin work on your essay. Manage your time carefully so that you can:

1. plan your essay

2. write your essay

3. revise and edit your final draft

Research Simulation

Informative Essay

Your Assignment

You will read three selections about animals that live in groups. Then you will write an informative essay on how and why the members of an animal group cooperate with each other.

Time Management: Informative Essay Task

Most formal writing tests are made up of two parts. Both parts of the tests are timed, so it's important to use your limited time wisely.

Part 1: Read Sources

35

Preview the Assignment

35 minutes

You will have 35 minutes to read three selections about animals that live in groups. You will then answer questions about the sources.

How Many?

How many pages of reading?

How many multiple-choice questions?

How many prose constructed-response questions?

How do you plan to use the 35 minutes?

Estimated time to read:

"The Crow Show"   minutes

"Gentle Giants"   minutes

"10-Ton Trouble"   minutes

Estimated time to answer questions?   minutes

Total   **35** minutes

> 35 minutes! That's not much time.

> Preview the questions. This will help you know which information you'll need to find as you read.

> This is a lot to do in a short time.

> Underline and take notes as you read. You probably won't have time to reread.

Part 2: Write the Essay

Plan and Write an Informative Essay

85 minutes

You will have 85 minutes to plan, write, revise, and edit your essay.

Your Plan

Before you start to write, decide on a main idea for your essay and details that support your main idea.

How do you plan to use the 85 minutes?

Estimated time for planning the essay? ⬚ minutes

Estimated time for writing? ⬚ minutes

Estimated time for editing? ⬚ minutes

Estimated time for checking spelling, grammar, and punctuation? ⬚ minutes

Total   **85 minutes**

> How much time do you have? Pay attention to the clock!

> Be sure to leave enough time for this step!

> Reread your essay, making sure that the points are clear. Check that there are no spelling or punctuation mistakes.

Your Assignment

You will read three texts about animals that live in groups. Then, you will write an informative essay about how and why the members of an animal group cooperate with each other.

Complete the following steps as you plan and compose your essay.

1. Read three informational articles about different animals.

2. Answer questions about the sources.

3. Plan, write, and revise your essay.

Part 1 (35 minutes)

You will now read the sources. Take notes on important facts and details as you read. You can refer to the sources and your notes as you write your essay.

The Crow Show

by Ned Cobb

Most of the year, crows live in family groups of up to 15 birds. They work together to help look after mothers, feed chicks, and defend the nest. In winter, crows gather together at night in roosts. Some roosts have fewer than 100 birds in a roost, and some have more than a million birds.

Crows have different duties to perform in their group. Guards watch for danger and warn
10   other crows. Scouts make sure that the way is safe when the group travels for food. Crows use many different calls. They warn of danger, express distress, ask for an assembly, and make threats. They even mimic other birds.

Crows often mob an enemy such as an owl or a hawk. The group flies at it, screeching and attempting to scare it away. Crows even mob humans—but only ones that they know are their enemies. And a crow will always
20   remember a person who has threatened it. As time passes, more and more crows will recognize and mob that person. Somehow, they describe their enemies to other crows. They also describe their friends! Someone who feeds crows regularly will soon have a fan club. They will be at the same place at the right time, and follow the person until they are fed.

Am I on Track?

Actual Time Spent Reading

Gentle Giants

by Marisol Martinez

Elephants live in groups of up to 25 animals. A group is a family of related females and their young. Males, after they leave the group at 12 to 15 years old, are no longer part of the group.

All the adult females in the group care for and raise new calves. However, elephants' concern isn't limited to newborns. Elephants take care of all members of their family. One group of elephants was observed that had
10 a member with a broken leg that had never healed. The group never traveled very fast, as they were making sure that the wounded animal could keep up.

A family of elephants is led by one of the oldest females. She makes decisions about much of the group's behavior. The leader remembers where to find water, food, and shelter, and warns the others of any dangers. If a predator comes close to a group, all of the
20 adults turn to face it, defending the young elephants that stay behind them.

People say that an elephant never forgets, and it is true that elephants are very intelligent. Elephants remember one another, and show great joy when they meet up. Reunited elephants will run toward each other as they

yell and trumpet. Their happiness to see each other again is obvious. An elephant's memory is also key to survival. Remembering every
30 route to sources of food and water allows the leader to safely guide the family over long distances.

The cooperation among the elephants in a group is amazing, but the bonds between a mother elephant and her child are even stronger. The mother stays with her child, helps it, defends it, bathes it, and guides it. The close relationship between a mother elephant and her daughter can last for 50 years.

Am I on Track?

Actual Time Spent Reading

10-Ton Trouble

by Yuen Lee Kwan

Killer whales are also known as orcas. They live in family groups called pods, with up to 40 animals. Some pods stay in the same place, and generally hunt fish. Other pods travel, and hunt sea mammals such as seals or penguins. Killer whales work together to hunt food.

Like bats, killer whales use sound to find their prey. They make clicks that travel through the water and bounce off objects. They can tell where something is, what shape it is, and how big it is.

Members of a pod often herd fish into one spot, and then they each feed in turn. When pods hunt mammals, one or more killer whales may slide onto the shore, scaring their prey into the water. That is where the other members of the pod are waiting.

Hunting isn't the only example of cooperation among killer whales. A pod has a female leader, and she and her children stay together all their lives. Mothers take good care of their young, and other members of the pod often babysit. No one has ever reported violent behavior between killer whales in the wild. Pod members have such close relationships that they always know where each other member is.

Am I on Track?

Actual Time Spent Reading

Questions

Answer the following questions. You may refer to your reading notes. Your answers to these questions will be scored. You will be able to refer to your answers as you write your essay in Part 2.

1 The word *predator* is used in "Gentle Giants." What word has the same meaning as *predator*?

   a. hunter

   b. female

   c. friend

   d. invalid

2 Which words best help the reader understand the meaning of *predator*?

   a. "A family of elephants is led by one of the oldest females."

   b. "... a member with a broken leg that had never healed."

   c. "... adults turn to face it, defending the young elephants ..."

   d. "... show great joy when they meet up."

3 Which claim could one make after reading these selections?

   a. Crows use sound to locate food.

   b. An elephant stays with her daughters for the rest of her life.

   c. Killer whales travel long distances to find fish.

   d. Only older males stay with elephant groups..

4 Which evidence below bests supports your answer to Question 3?

   a. "Crows use many different calls."

   b. "Elephants take care of all members of their family."

   c. "The close relationship ... can last for 50 years."

   d. "Like bats, killer whales use sound to find their prey."

Part 2 (85 minutes)

You now have 85 minutes to review your notes and sources and to plan, draft, revise, and edit your essay. You may use your notes and refer to the sources, but your essay must represent your original work. You may refer to your responses to the questions in Part 1, but you cannot change those answers. Now read your assignment and begin your work.

Your assignment

You have read three sources about animals that live in groups. The three texts are:

- "The Crow Show"
- "Gentle Giants"
- "10-Ton Trouble"

Think about the information on animal groups and their behavior.

Write an essay that explains how and why the members of an animal group cooperate with each other. Remember to use textual evidence to develop your topic.

Now begin work on your essay. Manage your time carefully so that you can:

1. plan your essay

2. write your essay

3. revise and edit your final draft

Response to Literature

Your Assignment

You will read the excerpt "The Wooden Horse" from *Tales from the Odyssey.* Then you will use what you have read to write a response to literature about how Odysseus and his men use a plan to trick the Trojans.

Time Management: Response to Literature Task

There are two parts to most formal writing tests. Both parts of the tests are timed, so it's important to use your limited time wisely.

Part 1: Read the Source

35

Preview the Assignment

35 minutes!
That's not
much time.

35 minutes

You will have 35 minutes to read an excerpt from *Tales of the Odyssey* about how Odysseus and his men trick the Trojans. You will then answer questions about the source.

How Many?

Preview the
questions.
This will
help you
know which
information
you'll need
to find as
you read.

How many pages of reading?

How many multiple-choice questions?

How many prose constructed-response questions?

How do you plan to use the 35 minutes?

Underline and
take notes as
you read. You
probably won't
have time to
reread.

Estimated time to read:

"The Wooden Horse"
from *Tales from the Odyssey*

This is a lot
to do in a
short time.

minutes

Estimated time to answer questions?

minutes

Total   **35** minutes

Part 2: Write the Essay

Plan and Write a Response to Literature

85 minutes

You will have 85 minutes to plan, write, revise, and edit your response to literature.

Your Plan

Before you start to write, determine the main idea of your response to literature and the details that support your main idea.

How do you plan to use the 85 minutes?

Estimated time for planning the essay? ☐ minutes

Estimated time for writing? ☐ minutes

Estimated time for editing? ☐ minutes

Estimated time for checking spelling, grammar, and punctuation? ☐ minutes

Total 85 minutes

> How much time do you have? Pay attention to the clock!

> Be sure to leave enough time for this step!

> Reread your essay, making sure that the points are clear. Check that there are no spelling or punctuation mistakes.

Your Assignment

> You will read an excerpt from *Tales from the Odyssey* and then write a response to literature explaining how Odysseus and his men use a plan to trick the Trojans.

Complete the following steps as you plan and compose your response to literature.

1. Read an excerpt from *Tales from the Odyssey*.

2. Answer questions about the source.

3. Plan, write, and revise your response to literature.

Part 1 (35 minutes)

You will now read the source. Take notes on important details as you read. You can refer to the source and your notes as you write your essay.

"The Wooden Horse"
from Tales from the Odyssey

By Mary Pope Osborne

For the next ten years, Odysseus camped with a thousand Greek warriors outside the walls of Troy. He despaired that the war would ever end. The Greeks slew many Trojan leaders in battle, including the prince who had stolen Helen from her Greek husband. But Helen herself remained captive within the thick walls of Troy. The Greeks had not been able to find a way to enter the city and take her back.

10 One day, Odysseus left the Greek camp and sat alone on the Trojan shore. He mourned the separation from his wife and felt terribly sad that he had missed seeing his son grow up. He feared that his mother and father might have died while he was at war, and that he would never lay eyes on them again.

Suddenly, a tall woman appeared before Odysseus. She wore a shining helmet and carried a spear and shield. The woman was
20 Athena, the goddess of wisdom and war and a daughter of Zeus.

Athena stared at Odysseus with flashing gray eyes. Though her gaze was fierce, it was also kind. Athena had always been fond of Odysseus. She admired his skills as a carpenter and craftsman. And she loved him for his strength and clever ways.

Odysseus was speechless as he stood before the goddess.

30   "I have come to help you take Helen back from the Trojans," she said. "Here is how you shall bring down the walls of Troy. Direct your carpenters to build a giant wooden horse. Hide with a few of your men inside the horse while the rest of the Greeks pretend to leave the island in defeat. Thinking the horse has been abandoned, the Trojans will bring it inside their walls. When night falls and the Greek soldiers return, open the gates of the city and

40 let them in."

The goddess then left as quickly as she had come.

Odysseus set to work at once. He called for his best carpenter and directed him to build the giant wooden horse. When the horse was finished, Odysseus ordered his men to carve Athena's name into its side. He then chose his bravest warriors and led them up a rope ladder to a secret trapdoor in the belly of the horse.

50 He and his men locked themselves inside and waited.

Soon Odysseus heard the Greek warriors set fire to their camp. He heard them board their ships and sail away in the night.

Odysseus dared not sleep as he waited for morning. After many hours, he heard seagulls crying in the dawn light. Then he heard footsteps on the sand and voices.

"What is this horse?" a Trojan shouted.
60 "Why did the Greeks build it, and then abandon it on our shore?"

"It is ours now!" said another. "Let us haul it inside our walls!"

"No, we must not!" cried another. "We must never trust gifts from the Greeks! Throw this monstrous thing into the sea!"

"Burn it!" some yelled.

"Let it stay!" others shouted.

The argument was interrupted by a Greek
70 soldier who had stayed behind and allowed himself to be captured by the Trojans. Now he claimed to be a traitor to the Greeks.

"This horse is a gift for Athena," he lied. "See her name carved into its side? If you destroy it, the goddess will punish you. But if you give it a place of honor in your city, she will give Troy power over all the world."

The Trojans argued bitterly about whether or not to trust the captive. Finally, the king
80 made a decision. "We will keep the wooden horse," he said. "Bring it inside the gates of Troy."

Odysseus felt great relief and excitement. Athena's plan was working! He and his men scarcely breathed as the Trojans heaved the giant horse onto rollers, then pushed it into the city.

Notes

Odysseus waited patiently for night to come. When all was silent, he opened the trapdoor in
90 the horse's belly.

It was pitch-black outside. The city was eerily calm. All the Trojans had returned to their homes and gone to bed.

Under the cover of darkness, Odysseus led the way down the rope ladder. He and his men crept to the city gates, unbolted them, and threw them open.

Hordes of Greek warriors were waiting on the other side! In the darkness, they had sailed
100 back to Troy and silently gathered outside the gates.

With a horrifying battle cry, the Greek army rushed into the city. They killed many men and captured women and children to keep as slaves. They found Helen and returned her to her Greek husband.

By dawn, the entire city of Troy was in flames. The triumphant Greek warriors loaded their ships with treasure. Then finally, after ten
110 long years, they set sail for home.

As a strong wind carried Odysseus and his twelve sleek ships away from the shores of Troy, he was jubilant. He imagined all of Ithaca rejoicing over his victorious return. He imagined himself soon embracing his beloved wife and son, and his parents. Never had he felt so hopeful and happy.

Am I on Track?

Actual Time Spent Reading

Questions

Answer the following questions. You may refer to your reading notes, and you should cite text evidence in your responses. Your answers to these questions will be scored. You will be able to refer to your answers as you write your response to literature in Part 2.

❶ What choice has the same meaning as the word *abandon* in line 60?

    a. put together

    b. turn around

    c. bring inside

    d. leave behind

❷ **Prose Constructed-Response** Why does Odysseus want to trick the Trojans?

_____

_____

_____

❸ **Prose Constructed-Response** Why does the Greek soldier need to be captured by the Trojans for the Greeks' plan to work?

_____

_____

_____

_____

Part 2 (85 minutes)

You now have 85 minutes to review your notes and the source and to plan, draft, revise, and edit your essay. While you may use your notes and refer to the source, your essay must represent your original work. You may refer to your responses to the questions in Part 1, but you cannot change those answers. Now read your assignment and begin your work.

Your assignment

You have read "The Wooden Horse" from *Tales from the Odyssey*.

Write a response to literature that explains how Odysseus and his men use a plan to trick the Trojans.

Now begin work on your essay. Manage your time carefully so that you can:

1. plan your essay

2. write your essay

3. revise and edit your final draft

Research Simulation

Narrative

Your Assignment

You will read two texts about the Oregon Trail. Then you will write a narrative about a historical trip on the Oregon Trail, as experienced by a child making the journey.

Time Management: Narrative Task

Most formal writing tests are made up of two parts. Both parts of the tests are timed, so it's important to use your limited time wisely.

Part 1: Read Sources

35

Preview the Assignment

35 minutes

You will have 35 minutes to read two selections about the Oregon Trail. You will then answer questions about the sources.

How Many?

How many pages of reading?

How many multiple-choice questions?

How many prose constructed-response questions?

How do you plan to use the 35 minutes?

Estimated time to read:

"The Oregon Trail" _____ minutes

"Pack Carefully" _____ minutes

Estimated time to answer questions? _____ minutes

Total 35 minutes

35 minutes! That's not much time.

Preview the questions. This will help you know which information you'll need to find as you read.

This is a lot to do in a short time.

Underline and take notes as you read. You probably won't have time to reread.

Part 2: Write the Narrative

Plan and Write a Narrative

85 minutes

You will have 85 minutes to plan, write, revise, and edit your story.

Your Plan

Before you start to write, determine the information from the sources you will use as a basis for your story. Then decide what will happen in your story.

How do you plan to use the 85 minutes?

Estimated time for planning the story? ☐ minutes

Estimated time for writing? ☐ minutes

Estimated time for editing? ☐ minutes

Estimated time for checking spelling, grammar, and punctuation? ☐ minutes

Total   **85** minutes

> How much time do you have? Pay attention to the clock!

> Be sure to leave enough time for this step!

> Reread your story, making sure that the points are clear. Check that there are no spelling or punctuation mistakes.

Your Assignment

> You will read two texts and then write a narrative about a child's experiences on the Oregon Trail.

Complete the following steps as you plan and compose your narrative.

1. Read an informational article about the Oregon Trail.

2. Read a fact sheet about the supplies pioneers brought with them on the Oregon Trail.

3. Answer questions about the sources.

4. Plan, write, and revise your story.

Part 1 (35 minutes)

You will now read the sources. Take notes on important facts and details as you read. You can refer to the sources and your notes as you write your story.

The Oregon Trail

By Arnold Douglas

In 1804, Lewis and Clark explored Oregon Country to make sure it was suitable for settlement. However, the journey was very difficult. At the time, no one knew of an easy way for people to travel there. Then in 1812, Robert Stuart made the 2,000 mile trip from Fort Astoria, in Oregon, to St. Louis, Missouri. This was an easier trail to travel. The trail that Robert Stuart traveled would become known as
10 the Oregon Trail.

Many years went by. Wagons weren't used on the Oregon Trail until 1836, when a missionary party made the journey. This proved that families could travel on the trail using wagons. So, in May 1843, a group of almost 1,000 people planned to travel west to Oregon Country from Independence, Missouri. Many of these people were farmers who believed that the land in Oregon would be
20 better than the land they currently farmed.

The group was led by Peter Burnett. Jesse Applegate was the leader of the groups of wagons and herds of livestock, which would travel more slowly than those traveling by foot or on horseback. Because many of those making the trip were farmers, they were ready for such a journey. They were used to taking care of livestock and wagons, and they were familiar with how to use axes and rifles.

30 Children of all ages traveled with their parents. Jesse Applegate's nephew, also named Jesse Applegate, was 7 years old when his family set out on the Oregon Trail.

The journey was challenging. People became sick from disease. They had to worry about food supplies and clean water, which eventually became very low. If a wagon lost a wheel or became damaged, it took time to repair it. Horses and oxen were lost to illness or injury.

40 It could be dangerous to cross a river with a wagon. To protect themselves from thieves, the travelers would draw their wagons into a circle at night. Sometimes they would place the horses and oxen inside this circle.

Even with these obstacles, the majority of people who set out on the trail made it to Oregon Country. They arrived six months after they set out, in November 1843. For many years after, groups set out to find prosperity

50 in Oregon Country, making the same journey along this trail as the pioneers in 1843.

Pack Carefully

Those traveling the Oregon Trail needed to spend at least $500 on supplies before they left. If animals and a wagon were needed, people could spend $1000 or more. A wagon was four feet by ten feet. Travelers would need to plan to bring enough food and supplies to last them for six months of travel. Wealthier families brought two wagons, one for food and one for other heavy supplies.

Inside a typical Oregon Trail pioneer's wagon, you would find about 1,000 pounds of food, including:

- 150–200 pounds of flour
- 30 pounds of bread
- 75 pounds of bacon
- 25 pounds of sugar
- 5 pounds of coffee beans
- 2 pounds of tea
- one bushel of dried fruit
- half a bushel of dried beans
- 10 pound of rice
- 10 pounds of salt
- 2 pounds of baking soda
- half a bushel of corn meal
- a bushel of corn
- spices
- a keg of pickles
- lard

Other items:

- cast iron pots and pans
- one or two kettles
- a Dutch oven
- a bed
- an axe
- a hatchet
- a small knife
- a handsaw
- 100 feet of rope
- a spade
- warm clothing
- blankets
- a rifle

Animals were important, to bring along, too. If a family could afford it, it would be wise to have:

- 4–6 oxen (the recommended number)
- a milk cow
- a pack horse
- a riding horse
- cattle
- a mule

Am I on Track?

Actual Time Spent Reading

Questions

Answer the following questions. You may refer to your reading notes, and you should cite text evidence in your responses. Your answers to these questions will be scored. You will be able to refer to your answers as you write your story in Part 2.

1 Why did many people want to make the trip along the Oregon Trail?

    a. They were did not like living in Missouri.

    b. They believed the farmland would be better in Oregon.

    c. They were bored and wanted to explore Oregon.

    d. They thought that Oregon would be a safe place to live.

2 **Prose Constructed-Response** Choose two details discussed in "The Oregon Trail" that might make traveling difficult.

_____

_____

_____

3 **Prose Constructed-Response** Travelers had to be selective about what they brought with them on their trip. Which items listed in "Pack Carefully" would be most important for someone to pack?

_____

_____

_____

_____

Part 2 (85 minutes)

You now have 85 minutes to review your notes and the source and to plan, draft, revise, and edit your narrative. While you may use your notes and refer to the source, your story must represent your original work. You may refer to your responses to the questions in Part 1, but you cannot change those answers. Now read your assignment and begin your work.

Your assignment

You have read two sources about the Oregon Trail. The two texts are:

- "The Oregon Trail"
- "Pack Carefully"

Write a narrative about a child's experience on the Oregon Trail.

Now begin work on your narrative. Manage your time carefully so that you can:

1. plan your story

2. write your story

3. revise and edit your final draft

Acknowledgments

Anansi and the Pot of Beans by Bobby and Sherry Norfolk. Copyright © 2006 by August House Publishers, Inc. Reprinted by permission of Marian Reiner on behalf of August House Publishers, Inc.

"Turtle Races with Beaver" from *Keepers of the Animals: Native American Stories and Wildlife Activities for Children* by Michael J. Caduto and Joseph Bruchac. Text copyright © 1991, 1997 by Michael J. Caduto and Joseph Bruchac. Reprinted by permission of Fulcrum Publishing, Inc.

"The Wooden Horse" excerpted and titled from *Tales from the Odyssey: Part One* by Mary Pope Osborne. Text copyright © 2002 by Mary Pope Osborne. Reprinted by permission of HarperCollins Publishers and Hyperion Books, an imprint of Disney Book Group.